To Dear Kip
With much love
from

12/3/07

Drawn from Life

Drawn from Life

The origins of famous characters in literature

Laurie Johnson

BANK HOUSE BOOKS

DRAWN FROM LIFE

First published 2007

ISBN 1-904408-24-9

Published by BANK HOUSE BOOKS

Designed and typeset in England by

BANK HOUSE BOOKS
PO Box 3
NEW ROMNEY TN29 9WJ
UK

NOTE:
Where copyright in photographs still exist every possible effort has been made to locate the owners of such copyright.

ABOUT THE AUTHOR
Laurie Johnson
Composer and Producer

His music is known worldwide: *The Avengers, The Professionals, This Is Your Life, Dr Strangelove*, concert works, stage musicals and much lese. What is not well known is his role as a producer, and the fact that he is also co-owner of Gainsborough Pictures and Mark 1 Productions, which was the first independent British television production company (*The New Avengers and The Professionals*), in addition to composing the music for them

In his autobiography, *Noises In The Head* (also published by BANK HOUSE BOOKS), he writes of a career in which he has worked with some of the greatest talents of the entertainment industry - Stanley Kubrick, Sir Peter Ustinov, Lord Bernard Miles and Lord Lew Grade; writers Lionel Bart, Herbert Kretzmer, Peter Cook and Dame Barbara Cartland; actors Sir Harry Secombe, Peter Sellers, Joanna Lumley, Dame Diana Rigg, Sir Spike Milligan, Beryl Reid, Kenneth Williams and James Coburn; as well as special-effects innovator, Ray Harryhausen.

He also writes of his legendary composer friends, Bernard Herrmann and Miklós Rósza, along with musicians, Ted Heath, Jack Parnell and Benny Green. Laurie Johnson founded The London Big Band which features most of the greatest jazz and orchestral musicians in Britain.

Contents

Introduction

That so many famous characters in literature were drawn from real life has long intrigued me. What was the inspiration that enabled so many writers to breathe such intense reality into imagined characters, and the power to propel them through entire novels? Some of the models were already well known to the writer, e.g. Charles Dickens whose father found fame as Mr Micawber in *David Copperfield.* Other models may be strangers in the street, anonymous beings who played upon Dickens's imagination.

Apart from the prodigious Charles Dickens, writers as diverse as Robert Louis Stevenson, Kenneth Grahame, Frank Richards (real name Charles Hamilton, the creator of Billy Bunter), Daphne du Maurier, W S Gilbert (of Gilbert and Sullivan), and Arthur Conan Doyle all drew inspiration from people, real people, who live on in their works, and so can never die. I have put together a modest collection of some of the characters in novels that have been 'drawn from life'. They have fascinated me and, I hope, will be of interest to others. In several instances, little known information came to me via unexpected routes from within the entertainment industry in my capacities as both composer and producer.

Robert Louis Stevenson

Long John Silver
Dr Jekyll and Mr Hyde

Lord Bernard Miles became a close friend and colleague after inviting me to compose the music for *Lock Up Your Daughters,* the musical for which he had written the 'book', with lyrics by the rising young songwriter Lionel Bart. The show opened the riverside Mermaid Theatre in the City of London in 1959. Bernard Miles, tireless and amusing, enjoyed a wide circle of friends, most of them drawn naturally from the worlds of plays, films and literature. Less expected, perhaps, in that circle was the former poet laureate John Masefield, whose masterpiece *Sea Fever* (*I Must Go Down To The Sea Again....*), every schoolboy was once required to learn by heart.

In 1962, at the age of 84 years, John Masefield wrote the following letter to Bernard Miles (then plain Mr. Miles) :

February the 12th, 1962

Dear Mr Miles,

Please, will you forgive my bothering you with what may seem a wearisome letter?

A friend has sent me the programme of your production of R.L. Stevenson's Treasure Island; and this makes me sure that you will not mind another lover of R.L.S. writing to you with this suggestion.

Would it be possible to arrange a Matinee in honour of the Teller of Tales on his Birthday in November, making it, in the main, a story-telling or recital, but in addition to the recitals of narrative poems, playing scenes from the plays, & causing some of the songs to be sung?

There are some less well known suggestions in his works that would come to startling life on the stage and there must still be thousands who love the work and would love to see it; & their children who are his to a child.

I grieve that I cannot see your Treasure Island; but hope that it has brought & will bring lots of pieces of eight to all hands.

Yours sincerely,
John Masefield

Telephone :
Clifton Hampden 77

BURCOTE BROOK. ABINGDON.

February the 12th. 1962.

Dear Mr Miles,

Please, will you forgive my bothering you with what may seem a wearisome letter?

A friend has sent me the programme of your production of R.L. Stevenson's <u>Treasure Island</u>; and this makes me sure that you will not mind another lover of R.L.S writing to you with this suggestion.

Would it be possible to arrange a Matinee in honour of the Teller of Tales on his Birthday in November, making it, in the main, a story-telling or recital, but in addition to the recitals of narrative poems, playing scenes from the plays, & causing some of the songs to be sung? There are some less well known suggestions in his works that would come to startling life on the stage; and there must still be thousands who love the work & would love to see it, in addition to the Scots in London, & the children who are his to a child.

I grieve that I cannot see your <u>Treasure Island</u>, but hope that it has brought & will bring lots of pieces of eight to all hands.

Yours sincerely.
John Masefield.

The original letter from John Masefield to Lord Bernard Miles (1962)

This letter was followed by Bernard's first meeting with Masefield at his home in the country, in order to discuss the theatrical tribute based on the writing of their common hero Robert Louis Stevenson.

Having spent the afternoon together discussing the project, which Masefield presented, he then walked his guest to the garden gate. They had got on so well that they dallied and continued to chat, meanwhile, Masefield's daughter had been preparing the evening meal, and after some delay she thought it prudent to alert her father to the fact that dinnertime had arrived. "Dad!' "Your dinner's ready!" echoed from within the house. Bernard and Masefield were still finding some more points of mutual interest, which simply had to be discussed. Again came the voice from within – a more urgent message "Daaad!" "Your dinner's getting cold!!" As even eminent poet laureates have to eat, Bernard took his leave. But Bernard was very amused at the thought of the unexpected contrast between the poetic flights of imagination "All I want is a tall ship and a star to sail her by"; and the down to earth "Dad, your dinner's getting cold!" from the practical flat tones of Masefield's daughter. This was the first of several further meetings. After the first meeting, Bernard was sent this letter by Masefield :

> Dear Mr Miles
>
> I am sending to you 9 typed pieces, each illustrating, fairly well, bits of RLS's life.
>
> I hope to send typed copies, early next week, of all the things and poems that should be picked from.
>
> Please, will you let me know, if you wish specially for copies of any of the things already suggested.?
>
> With my greetings to your wife and you.
>
> Yours sincerely,
> John Masefield.

Before Bernard died, he passed over to me, for safe keeping, various plans, plays and ideas which he had never got round to presenting at the Mermaid Theatre. One, which particularly interested me, was the celebration of the works of Robert Louis Stevenson that had been compiled by John Masefield.

One piece was intriguingly entitled: 'The Origin of the Hispaniola's Apple Barrel'.

When Stevenson's father, Thomas was a boy, he knew a man named Souter, who worked for his father (RLS's grandfather). The family, whose business was the design and building of lighthouses, owned a modest fleet of ships, used to call on their chain of coastal beacons. John Masefield had come across a piece written by Stevenson that recounted the two-faced nature of Souter's character, later to be transformed into his greatest creation Long John Silver in *Treasure Island.*

This is what RLS wrote: "The name of Souter has twice escaped my pen and I

Lord Bernard Miles

John Masefield

feel I owe him a vignette. Souter first attracted notice as mate of the *Praam* and the *Bell Rock*, and rose gradually to become Captain of *The Regent*. He was active, admirably skilled in his trade, and a man incapable of fear. So many perils shared, and the partial familiarity of so many voyages had given this man a strong hold in my grandfather's estimation; and there is no doubt that Souter had the art to court and please him with much hypocritical skill. He usually dined on Sundays in the cabin. He used to come down daily after dinner for a glass of port or whiskey, often in his full rig of sou'wester, oil skins, and long boots; and I have often heard it described how insultingly he carried himself on these appearances, artfully combining the extremes of deference with a blunt and seaman-like demeanour. My father and uncles, with the devilish penetration of the boy, were far from deceived; and my father, indeed, was favoured with an object lesson not to be mistaken. He crept one rainy night into an apple barrel on deck, and from this place of ambush overheard Souter and a comrade conversing in their oilskins. The smooth sycophant of the cabin had wholly disappeared, and the boy listened with wonder to a vulgar and truculent ruffian". This is clearly the source and inspiration of the scene in *Treasure Island* in which the two-faced Long John Silver plotting the mutiny on the deck of the Hispaniola, is overheard by Jim Hawkins, hiding in the apple barrel! As RLS wrote in *Treasure Island* 'Now, just after sundown, when all my (i.e. Jim Hawkin's) work was over, and I was on my way to my berth, it occurred to me that I should like an apple. I ran on deck. The watch was all forward looking out for island. The man at the helm was watching the luff of the sail and whistling away gently to himself; and that was the only sound accepting the swish of the sea against the bows and around the sides of the ship.

I got bodily into the apple barrel, and found there were scarce an apple left; but

Long John Silver, from a painting by Sue Randle

the sides of the ship.

I got bodily into the apple barrel, and found there were scarce an apple left; but sitting down there in the dark, what with the sound of the waters and the rocking movement of the ship, I had either fallen asleep, or was on the point of doing so, when a heavy man sat down with rather a clash close by. The barrel shook as he leaned his shoulder against it, and I was about to jump up when the man began to speak. It was Silver's voice, and, before I heard a dozen words, I would not have shown myself for all the world, but lay there, trembling and listening, in the extreme of fear and curiosity; for from these dozen words I understood that the lives of all the honest men on board depended on me alone…..

…….. You may imagine how I felt when I heard this abominable old rogue addressing another in the very same words of flattery as he had used to myself. I think if I had been able, that I would have killed him through the barrel. Meantime, he ran on, little supposing he was overheard."

I hadn't heard this story before and haven't heard it repeated since. But perhaps one of my readers has?

RLS's decision to create Long John Silver with his left leg missing was prompted by the unfortunate example of his friend and collaborator, the writer W.E. Henley, had lost his left leg a decade before *Treasure Island* was written. Due to diabetes Henley was compelled to have his left leg amputated below the knee, to be replaced by a wooden limb. To quote Stevenson's description of Silver 'his left leg was cut off close by the hip and he was given no wooden leg'. The fact that RLS made Silver eschew – a wooden leg adds another dimension of independence to his creation of an already rugged and powerful figure, which indeed Souter was.

The 'apple barrel' incident with RLS's father, when a boy, convinces me, and the fact that Stevenson chose a six letter name starting with an 'S' and ending with an 'R'.

S-o-u-t-e-R — S-i-l-v-e-R!

Dr Jekyll and Mr Hyde

Born in Edinburgh in 1850, Robert Louis Stevenson was always a sickly, consumptive child. Brought up, mainly, by a devoted Scottish nanny named Alison Cunningham, RLS later wrote of himself, "He was from a child an ardent and uncomfortable dreamer. When he had a touch of fever at night, the night-hag would have him by the throat and pluck him, strangling and screaming, from his sleep." His 'brownies', as he called his dreams, fed his fevered imaginings with images of death and damnation. Feelings of guilt would haunt RLS all his life.

Despite a strict, genteel upbringing, he was drawn, as a young man, to the seediest parts of Edinburgh. Under the pseudonym of "Velvet Coat" he became a familiar figure in the drinking dens and brothels of the city.

"I felt younger, lighter, happier in body; within I was conscious of a heady recklessness, a current of disordered sensual images running like a mill-race in my fancy. I knew myself, at the first breath of this new life, to be more wicked, ten-fold more wicked, sold a slave to my original evil; and the thought in that moment braced and delighted me like wine." These were the thoughts RLS transferred to the character of Dr. Jekyll in his greatest and most original masterpiece *Dr. Jekyll and Mr Hyde.*

He had been advised by doctors to move to sunnier, more southerly Bournemouth. With his wife, Fanny Osbourne, and his stepson, Lloyd, RLS settled into the genteel society of that quiet resort. His illness continued to dominate his life and work and, indeed, the lives of those around him. He had been fascinated, as a child, by the case of Deacon Brodie, outwardly a respectable Edinburgh cabinetmaker, but in fact a leader of a gang of burglars and criminals. Stevenson's nurse had captured the boy's imagination with stories of this wicked man, who was eventually hanged for his villainy, made worse, in her eyes, by his hypocritical pretences of churchgoing respectability.

When RLS's startling *Jekyll and Hyde* novel did start to manifest itself, it came to him in his sleep. His wife found him tossing and turning, crying out in horror in his bed. When she awakened him he was irate. "Why did you wake me? I was dreaming a fine bogey tale!" His 'brownies' had been at work. Fanny called the doctor to him the next day. "I found my 'shilling shocker'" cried RLS excitedly. He hoped the success of the yet unwritten book would solve all his financial problems. He worked ferociously, sitting up in bed, his pen driven across the paper at great speed, as though possessed. The household was respectfully quiet. "We all went about in a tip-toeing silence", wrote his son-in-law, Lloyd. "Passing Stevenson's door, I would see him sitting up in bed, filling page after page, and apparently never pausing for a moment."

Astonishingly, the book was completed in three days, but this manuscript was not destined to be the final book, as we know it today. For when Fanny read the manuscript she accused him of missing the point, of reducing a potential masterpiece into a sensational pot-boiler. In his anger and disappointment Stevenson burned the manuscript. We shall never know which elements of the original draft remain, or were replaced. Were some passages too revealing, too shocking? The answers to these questions went up in flames. Yet, amazingly he re-wrote the entire book in a further three days. The inspiration for it had come to him in his sleep… sleep heavily induced by a draft of an opiate made up for him by a chemist in Westbourne. We know from the book that Dr. Jekyll's transformation to his 'otherself' occurred through his imbibing a mind-altering potion.

I had read that the obliging chemist worked in a pharmacy, the rear of which was covered by a domed glass roof. On a visit to Bournemouth, I resolved to retrace Stevenson's steps from his house in Alum Chine, called 'Skerryvore' (after one of the lighthouses built by his family) via the Victorian Arcade to a likely chemist's shop. I enquired of the young lady, behind the counter, if the shop had been a Chemist's for many years. She screwed up her face and replied thoughtfully "Yeah, think so!" This was enough for me. Unobserved, I slipped into the room at the rear of the shop and, sure enough, there was the Victorian domed glass roof overhead. So this was the place where the draft had been prepared, the heady, heavy brew that released all the guilt-ridden experiences stored in his subconscious since childhood.

When he was able to work, out of his sick bed, Stevenson had the habit of pacing his room, waiting for inspiration to arrive. This practice was well known and the painter John Singer Sargent captured this in his famous portrait of RLS. 'Skerryvore', the house, was bombed during the Second World War. Only the outlines of the original walls remain. The site has been transformed into a memorial garden to Stevenson. I visited 'Skerryvore', and found that grass turf had been laid between the ruined walls outlining the various rooms of the house, giving the illusion of fitted carpets. I imagined RLS pacing up and down these very spaces. RLS would also pace around the small courtyard of the house, awaiting the arrival of inspiration. He described himself as "like a weevil in a biscuit".

Portrait of Robert Louis Stevenson painted by John Singer Sargent

Dr Jekyll and Mr Hyde from a painting by Sue Randle

Maybe there is – or was - something in the air of Bournemouth. How else explain the strange fact is that the two greatest, groundbreaking psychological novels in English literature — *Mary Shelley's Frankenstein* and RLS's *The Strange Case of Dr. Jekyll and Mr Hyde* — were both created within a few miles of each other along England's genteel southern coast?

In the novel, Dr. Jekyll had to drink a potion in order to become his 'otherself'. But, gradually the draft had no further effect over the two conflicting identities; they changed places unbidden, as they have always done – the original sin in all men. That was Stevenson's allegory.

Both Dr. Jekyll and Mr Hyde were the tortured author himself.

J.M. Barrie

Peter Pan   Mary Rose

JM Barrie was already an established writer when he conceived the notion of his now famous children's classic. Inspiration came from an unexpected source. Barrie, renowned as the writer of *The Admirable Crichton*, lived in a house on Bayswater Road in London, right across the road from Kensington Gardens. He was in the habit of exercising his St. Bernard dog, Portos, in the gardens every day. One day he met three little boys in the charge of their nanny. The boys were drawn to the big dog and they played games together. Portos's owner also intrigued them – a strange little man in a bowler hat and a long overcoat, who smoked a pipe continuously and coughed a lot. He amused the boys. He could pull funny faces, roll his eyebrows and waggle his ears. He told them stories about the fairies and the "little folk" who lived in Kensington Gardens. All this intrigued the boys and Barrie started to meet up with them in the park almost every day, after school.

Then, by coincidence, Barrie and his wife, Mary, were guests at a soiree one evening, and sitting next to them was a couple who were talking about their three little boys. Barrie overheard the conversation and introduced himself as the man with the big dog in Kensington Gardens. The parents of the three brothers were Arthur and Sylvia Llewellyn Davies. Arthur was a lawyer in the City and Sylvia was the sister of the great actor/manager Gerald du Maurier. All four adults got on well and a strong friendship was formed. The bonding element was, of course, the boys – Peter, Jack, George. They also had a baby brother Michael, who was to become an important element in the story.

Barrie was well known for elements of whimsy in some of his writings, but nothing to equal what would become his most famous story, *Peter Pan.* He became a frequent visitor to the Llewellyn Davies home, often calling for tea with Sylvia and the boys. He was becoming so attached to the boys that his behaviour began to be resented by their father, although he accepted Barrie's genuine affection for the boys, having no children of his own.

Barrie and his wife Mary had taken a cottage in Tilford, named Black Lake Cottage, for the summer, and they invited Llewellyn Davies family to join them for a holiday. The fourth son, baby Michael, was left at home with the nanny, Mary Hodgson. Barrie organised pirate games for the boys around the lake and adjoining forests. On their return to London the Llewellyn Davies family moved from 31 Kensington Park Gardens to number 25, a much larger house up the street to accommodate their growing family. The boys' nursery, on the second floor, was the inspiration for Barrie's *Peter Pan* nursery set design. The school which George, the eldest son, attended was in nearby Orme Square, just a little further down Bayswater Road from the Barrie house.

The Barrie's were both devastated by the loss of their dear dog, Portos, who had been like a child to them. A Newfoundland puppy, called Luath, took Portos's place. He had a habit of lying in wait for Barrie, and pouncing on him unexpectedly. Then would follow a kind of mad hide-and-seek chase all around the house, creating mayhem. This frantic game was called 'Mad Dog'.

Barrie had been working on a book called *The Little White Bird*, featuring three boys in Kensington Gardens. The book was published and sold in good numbers. It was the foundation for his great fairytale, gradually taking shape in his mind. He made notes, and started work on *Peter Pan* in November, 1903; it was completed some five months later.

Charles Frohman, the American producer, was eagerly awaiting Barrie's next play. So anxious was Barrie for Frohman to produce *Peter Pan* that he offered to give it to him, on condition that he would produce it along with another new play he had written. Their conversation went like this - "You know I have an agreement to deliver you the manuscript of a new play. Well, I have it all right, but I am sure it will not be a commercial success. But, it is a dream child of mine, and I am so anxious to see it on the stage that I have written another play, which I will be glad to give you, which will compensate you for any loss on the one I am so eager to see produced."

"Don't bother about that!" said Frohman. "I will produce both plays." Barrie hadn't expected Frohman, having read the play, to be so enthusiastic about it. The play was then titled *The Great White Father*. Frohman's suggestion of changing the title to *Peter Pan* was a masterstroke, and Barrie gladly accepted it.

By now, Michael, youngest of the Llewellyn Davies boys, was old enough to be included in the various get-togethers in Kensington Gardens, and the holidays at Black Lake Cottage. Barrie was becoming particularly fond of Michael. Meanwhile, the preparations for the London production of *Peter Pan* were gathering pace. Sylvia Llewellyn Davies's brother, Gerald, was contracted to play the dual roles of Captain Hook and Mr Darling, whose character was based on Arthur Llewellyn Davies. The boys visited the Duke of York's Theatre and were made a great fuss of by Barrie.

Proceedings were delayed so that the boys could experience the flying ballet (*George Kirby's Flying Ballet*). Kirby's were to engineer the illusion of the characters flying. An actor in a dog's costume, designed to be as much like Luath as possible, amused the boys with his antics, copying Luath's rolling gait while playing Nana, the dog in the nursery scenes of *Peter Pan*.

It was now, when Barrie felt most in need of the boys, that the blow fell. It was decided that the Llewellyn Davies family would move to an even larger house in distant Berkhamstead. As Arthur said pointedly at the time, "...twenty-five miles away from J M Barrie." Barrie was devastated, as various letters to the boys testify. He knew he was happier in the company of children — himself a boy who never grew up — than with adults, including his wife Mary. His idealised love and admiration for Sylvia was something else, and grew out of her being the mother of his idols, which put her on a pedestal apart.

Barrie was very sad without the boys in London, as shown in this letter he wrote to Peter - 'My dear Peter, sometimes when I walk in the gardens with Luath I see a vision and I cry "Hooray, there's Peter!" and then Luath barks joyously and we run to the vision, and then it turns out not to be Peter and just another boy, and then I cry like a water cart, and Luath hangs his sorrowful tail. Oh dear, how I wish you were here, then it would be London again.'

The opening night of *Peter Pan* on the 27th November 1904 was a great success, despite Barrie's doubts about its commercial appeal. At midnight, Frohman, in New York, received a cablegram from London '*Peter Pan* all right, looks like a big success'.

Sylvia and Arthur Llewellyn Davies, along with their boys George, Jack, Peter and Michael, with exception of the new baby Nico, all attended the first matinee after the opening night. They travelled to the theatre in a private bus, and were seated in one of the theatre boxes. Gerald du Maurier, as Captain Hook, was impressive and terrifying. After the performance the family went back to Barrie's home for tea, before returning to Berkhamstead.

Barrie was continuously revising *Peter Pan* for the American production, and went down to the cottage at Black Lake to work; Michael, his favourite, went also, accompanied by his mother. They stayed for two weeks, and Barrie was happy. He took photographs of Michael dressed as *Peter Pan*, which later would be given as a guide to Frampton, the sculptor of the *Peter Pan* statue.

James Barrie

Michael, dressed as *Peter Pan*

Arthur Llewellyn Davies became very ill with a horrendous cancer of the mouth, from which he eventually died. Barrie was very supportive financially, freely giving his time sitting with Arthur in hospital. After Arthur's death, Barrie took on all the financial responsibility of Sylvia and the boys. He installed the family in a new home in London, at 23 Camden Hill Square, not far from his own house.

It had taken from 1904 to 1909 for Barrie to adapt the play of *Peter Pan* into a book, which satisfied him. Its title was: *Peter Pan in Kensington Gardens*.

The original edition of *Peter Pan in Kensington Gardens* in 1909

Tragedy often touched the life of J M Barrie. After ten years of a failing marriage Mary Barrie divorced him. An aspiring dramatist, Gilbert Cannon, was named in the divorce proceedings. Two days after the divorce case ended, a major blow fell with the death of Sylvia. She had asked Barrie to take care of her boys. Barrie became their official guardian. Mary Hodgson, the boys' faithful nanny, continued to care for them in Camden Hill. Although she had somewhat resented Barrie in the past, she was grateful that he had carried out his responsibilities so dutifully and lovingly.

During the night of the 12th April 1912 the statue to Peter Pan, commissioned by Barrie, was secretly erected in Kensington Gardens.

Statue of Peter Pan, in Kensington Gardens

Barrie was not entirely happy with the expression of the face on the figure. "It doesn't show the devil in Peter."

The First World War broke out and George and Jack enlisted. Another blow fell when George was killed in action in France. Michael, highly intelligent, went to Oxford, all paid for, of course, by Barrie. Michael, the favourite, was rather inclined to take Barrie for granted. That Barrie loved all the boys was obvious. There has been conjecture over Barrie's sexuality. In later life, Nico said that if there had been any impropriety the family would have known about it. "He was an innocent, or he could never have written *Peter Pan*."

The final, terrible blow fell for Barrie in May 1921, when a reporter asked Barrie if he had heard the news, (he hadn't) that Michael and another Oxford undergraduate, Rupert Buxton, had both drowned in a pool while bathing. A double suicide was suspected. A possible homosexual pact to die together was suggested. Barrie, who knew that Michael couldn't swim, was inconsolable in his grief.

J M Barrie and Michael Llewellyn Davies

Mary Rose

In 1921, he put all his early thoughts and emotions about Sylvia's death into a ghost story, *Mary Rose*, in which a young mother is 'spirited away' on a visit to a Scottish island. She returns years later as a ghost to seek her son, but fails to recognise him as a grown man. A fascinating and atmospheric play, which so fascinated film director Alfred Hitchcock that he spent years trying to find a satisfactory way to bring it to the screen. My old friend, Bernard Herrmann, the composer who worked with Hitchcock on most of his greatest films, knew that Hitch was obsessed with the story, but predicted that he would never succeed in filming it because simply "He doesn't know how!" Another colleague, actor Gordon Jackson, told me that Hitchcock had approached him to record the entire dialogue of the story. Joining him in this enterprise was the original *Mary Rose*, the legendary Fay Compton. Even this recording could not unlock a formula for Hitchcock. Incidentally, I knew Fay Compton, who in later years lived near my home. We met quite often while exercising our dogs on the common near Grim's Dyke, one time home of W S Gilbert – more

of him later. Fay Compton had a Bassett Hound named Orson, after Orson Welles, who had given her the dog. She was responsible for my wife, Dot, and myself adding a Bassett Hound to our family of five dogs.

Hitchcock never did succeed in making a film of '*Mary Rose'*.

Sylvia Llewellyn Davies

Barrie wrote in his dedication to the Llewellyn Davies boys: '*Peter Pan* was made up from rubbing all five of you together". But there can be little doubt that he favoured Michael and, indeed, there is in *Peter Pan* something of 'the boy who never grew up', J M Barrie himself.

Based on what Barrie wrote and is known Sylvia Llewellyn Davies, the mother of the boys, was *Mary Rose*. Therefore, *Mary Rose* must have been the mother of *Peter Pan*, wasn't she?

Daphne Du Maurier

Mrs Danvers   Maxim de Winter

These are clear and obvious links between the last chapter, on *Peter Pan*, and the story of *Rebecca* and its celebrated author Daphne du Maurier.

Daphne had inherited her literary talent from her grandfather, George du Maurier, a hugely popular writer of plays and books (*Peter Ibbetson*, *Trilby*, etc.) He was also a gifted artist whose work was prominently displayed in *Punch*. Her father, Gerald du Maurier, became a legendary actor in his own lifetime, developing a revolutionary style of naturalistic acting which, it is said, overwhelmed and influenced gifted successors like Laurence Olivier and John Gielgud. Such performers broke with the overheated declamatory style that had been prevalent in the theatre since Victorian times. Gerald du Maurier had his own theatre in the West End, Wyndhams, and gathered around him an array of splendid talents. Many became household names. Du Maurier discovered, or encouraged, such luminaries as Gladys Cooper, Gertrude Lawrence, Charles Laughton, Basil Rathbone, Sir Cedric Hardwick, Edith Evans, Gordon Harker, Nigel Bruce and Raymond Massey.

Growing up in Hampstead, the young Daphne du Maurier met them all, or most of them. The family's Sunday dinners were regularly attended by the rising stars of her fathers' theatrical circle. She recalled with special admiration a man she called 'Uncle Basil' (Basil Rathbone), never dreaming that one day he would act in a film version of one of her books *Frenchman's Creek.*

Daphne personally witnessed her father's mesmerising performance as Captain Hook in *Peter Pan.* She saw the play, in the company of her cousins the Llewellyn Davies boys. Daphne recalled, "How Hook was hated, with his flourish, his poses, his dreaded diabolical smile! That ashen face, those blood red lips, the long, dark, greasy curls, the sardonic laugh, the maniacal scream, the appalling curtsey of gestures; and that above all most terrible of moments when he descended the stairs and with slow, merciless cunning poured the poison into Peter's glass. There was no peace in those days until the monster was destroyed, and the fight upon the pirate ship was a fight to the death. Gerald *was Hook*; he was no dummy dressed from Simmons' in a Clarkson wig, ranting and roaring about the stage, a grotesque figure whom the modern child finds a little comic. He was a tragic and rather ghastly creation, who knew no peace, and whose soul was in torment; a dark shadow; a sinister dream; a bogey of fear who lives perpetually in the grey recesses of every small boy's mind… and, because he had imagination and a spark of genius Gerald made him alive."

Performing the role of Hook proved a great strain on Gerald du Maurier — two four-hour performances every day! Daphne closely watched her father acting and directing his plays, recalling his advice to a young actor "Don't force it, don't be self conscious, do what you generally do any day of your life when you come into a room. Bite your nails, yawn, lie down on the sofa and read a book – do anything or nothing, but don't look dramatically at the audience and speak with one eye on the right-hand box. If you must look in front of you, stare right at the back of the pit, as though nobody was there." Daphne was impressed by her father's new visions of acting styles. Gerald, in turn, returned his daughter's deep regard. Although she was one of three daughters, she was certainly her fathers' favourite. She, too, lived in a world of imagination. The rest of the family noted her creative flights, as fictional characters formed in her mind "Daphne's showing off again", they would say.

The closeness between father and daughter was remarkable. It was known that Gerald had wanted a son, and Daphne wanted to be that son. She had some masculine traits of thought and behaviour that she called 'the boy in the box'. She preferred men's jackets, heavy pullovers, and corduroy trousers, to the flowing, floaty garments favoured by her sisters. Gerald dedicated a poem to her that is quite revealing:

My very slender one
So brave of heart, but delicate of will
So careful not to wound, never kill
My tender one –
Who seems to live in kingdoms all her own
In realms of joy
When heroes young and old
In climates hot and cold
Do deeds of daring and much fame
And she knows she could do the same
If only she'd been born a boy
And sometimes in the silent of night
I wake and think perhaps my darling's right
And that she should have been
And if I'd had my way
She would have been, a boy.

Daphne with her father, Gerald du Maurier

My very slender one
So feminine and fair, so fresh and sweet
So full of fun and womanly deceit.
My tender one, who seems to dream her life away alone
A daunting girl
But always well attired
And loves to be admired
Wherever she may be, and wants
To be the being who enchants
Because she has been born a girl.
And sometimes in the turmoil of the day
I pause, and think my darling may
Be one of those who will
For good or ill
Remain a girl for ever, and be still
A girl.

Strange thoughts, indeed, implying that his favourite daughter might be more suited to being a boy. When Daphne started to have her writing published, Gerald was very proud that his own father's writing skills seemed to be reborn in his gifted daughter. When he read *The Loving Spirit* in 1932 he was shocked at some of its daring love scenes. When Daphne started to have boyfriends, Gerald did not disguise his jealousy. When the young film director, Carol Reed, appeared on the scene, Gerald's jealousy intensified. If she was out for the evening with Reed Gerald waited up for her return, positioning himself at the top of the staircase so that he could look down through the window above the front door to see her arrive home. He was angry. He became bullying and sarcastic. Daphne turned cold against her father, became more than ever determined to go her own way.

Gerald was not destined to live long enough to witness the success of Daphne's early novels *Jamaica Inn* and *Rebecca*. *Rebecca* sold forty-five thousand copies in its first month. David O. Selznick, the prominent Hollywood producer, was quick to buy bought the film rights. The composer Bernard Herrmann told to me an amusing story about Selznick. "Hitchcock was a great practical joker. After he had read *Rebecca* he wrote to Selznick suggesting, apparently seriously, that since the novel was written in the first person he felt that the title of the movie version should be called DAPHNE! Selznick hit the roof when he received Hitch's memo. "D'ya think I've paid a fortune to buy the rights to a world bestseller known everywhere as *Rebecca*, for you to change its title to DAPHNE?!!" Here Bernard Herrmann chuckled at the recollection of this story. The solemn Selznick hadn't appreciated that the puckish Hitchcock was pulling his leg.

Maxim de Winter

Laurence Olivier was cast in the role of Maxim de Winter, the troubled hero of Hitch's movie of *Rebecca*. Joan Fontaine was cast as the heroine, the second Mrs de Winter, whose first name is never once revealed in the novel or the film. Olivier had campaigned for his wife, Vivien Leigh, to be given the role, but Selznick's instincts told him that the heroine needed to be unsophisticated, easily intimidated. Joan Fontaine had these qualities. Vivien Leigh did not. Olivier's resentment overflowed into his overbearing performance as Maxim de Winter.

It is clear that de Winter's domineering attitude towards his awkward young bride was not without its real-life parallels in Gerald du Maurier's behaviour towards Daphne at the time of her association with Carol Reed in a key scene in the film, for instance, de Winter belittles and mocks his vulnerable wife in front of the cruel housekeeper Mrs Danvers over a trivial matter of a broken china ornament.

Gerald du Maurier

Sir Laurence Olivier as Maxim de Winter in Alfred Hitchcock's film of *Rebecca*

Mrs Danvers

There is a further unspoken mystery surrounding the relationship between the late, first Mrs de Winter — Rebecca — and the possessive Mrs Danvers. A strong lesbian influence is discernable beneath the surface. Daphne was aware of it, but did not spell it out. Yet it was there nonetheless, for those who cared to see it. Daphne's own bisexuality, which she termed her 'Venetian tendencies', is reflected in those memorable sequences.

Mrs Danvers was based on a lesbian schoolteacher, Mlle Fernande Yvon, at a French boarding school that Daphne, aged seventeen, attended for three terms. By the end of the last term Daphne and the teacher, whose tendencies Daphne described as 'Venetian', had become intimate friends. They loved each other "in every conceivable way". Throughout her life Daphne enjoyed 'Venetian' friendships, actress Gertrude Lawrence amongst them.

In 1932, Daphne married Major Frederick Browning (later General). They had three children, two girls and a boy, and, according to daughter Flavia, they shared a very happy family life in Daphne's beloved Cornwall.

Joan Fontaine (Mrs de Winter), Sir Laurence Olivier (Maxim de Winter) and Judith Anderson (Mrs Danvers) from the film of *Rebecca* directed by Alfred Hitchcock.

Frank Richards (Charles Hamilton)

Frank Richards

Billy Bunter and Co.

Denis Preston, the first independent record producer in the UK, in addition to his highly successful popular recordings of artists such as Acker Bilk, Cleo Laine, Lonnie Donnegan, Roger Whittaker, etc., in contrast he recorded the voices of several eminent literary figures such as Aldous Huxley and W H Auden. Denis and I were partners in various recording projects, so I was aware of his literary interests.

We shared an enthusiasm for the stories of Frank Richards (real name Charles Hamilton), the creator of Billy Bunter and co. of Greyfriars School. Hamilton's stories, published in boys' magazines like *The Magnet* and *The Gem* were enormously popular in the inter-war years, and transferred successfully to stage and television.

Denis Preston invited Charles 0Hamilton to write a School song — in Latin! — for Greyfriars School, I composed the music. Denis also recorded Charles Hamilton's reminiscences about his literary creations and general attitude to life. I can do no better than quote him fairly extensively.

Charles Hamilton said: "Bunter is a combination of three persons. His circumference was borrowed from an editor; he overflowed the arms of his armchair! How he ever got into that chair and out of it again I never knew, but his circumference struck me very strongly and I handed it onto Bunter. Another source was a relation of mine, who used to peer at me through his spectacles, like an owl, that's where Bunter got his specs. Another relative was always expecting a cheque which never arrived, in the meanwhile, he was very anxious to borrow a pound – that became Bunter's postal order!" Charles Hamilton's continues: "There used to be,

when I was a kid, something called Bunter's Nervine, some kind of quack medicine; I never came across it but I used to see it advertised and that must have put the name in my mind. And, also, the words Billy Bunter suggest someone who is fairly plump.

Billy Bunter was invented, if you can call it invented, as far back as 1899. I had to see an editor then, and I took him several sketches then, and amongst them was Bunter, and he looked them all over and chose something else. So, I slipped Bunter back into my coat pocket and that was that. He remained in cold storage for nearly nine years, then one day, *The Gem* Editor called me up to the office and told me he was starting a new paper, and I was to write for it. And I said I would, and did, and then, when I was doing the first number I remembered my old Bunter, so I just inserted him in the first story. He was a very minor character to begin with. Bunter is certainly the stupidest boy in the Remove, and he has rather a gift of cunning, he's simple, but at the same time a little sly, always unsuccessful. Bunter's greediness has no limit. He is very fond of jam, very fond of jam tarts, cake, buns, éclairs and everything else in the edible line. Bunter wanders from the truth without realising what he is doing. He doesn't realise he is a liar, he's very indignant if his word is doubted, very indignant indeed. The other fellows call them fibs or crammers, but it's understood that Bunter is not conscious of being a liar, or being a young rascal, he's a very fine fellow, in fact he thinks he's really the only decent fellow at Greyfriars and all the rest are more or less beasts.

When Bunter rolled casually off the typewriter in 1908, I couldn't have foreseen he'd still be talked about in 1961, never crossed my mind for a moment. What I should do without him, I really don't know? Sometimes I can hardly believe that there isn't a boy called Bunter. It's hard to believe that he doesn't exist".

Charles Hamilton spoke about other famous characters at Greyfriars. "Herbert

Vernon-Smith has some very good qualities; he's got plenty of pluck, and he'll stick to anybody in a jam, and he's capable, and he's a good man at games, he's reckless, headstrong, self willed, he's given to gambling and backing horses, and when he gets across to France he plays in the casino. Oh, I had a long gambling campaign there once. Stayed about three months. I was in the casino every afternoon and evening, or nearly every one. I remember I had to stick my editors for some cheques in advance to see me through; when it was over I had just enough money to pay my hotel bill and hire a car to get off into Italy. If you're going to write stories you must know the subject you are going to write about; what's the use of warnings against gambling if you don't know what gambling is.

Hurree Jamset Ram Singh: "I liked the idea of making a coloured boy a friend on equal terms with the other boys, and a valued member of the company. Well, I thought it had a good effect. No end of readers in India liked it, of course, though they sometimes raised objection to the boy's English. I

had a letter from an Indian schoolmaster, who told me he had never heard any Indian speak English precisely as Hurree Jamset Ram Singh. I've no doubt he was right. It's made comical on purpose, but it isn't a complete invention. So far as my acquaintance with them goes, Hindus do sometimes make the most extraordinary blunders in English. For instance, a Hindu once said to me, back in the early 1890's, "Top of a beautiful morning!" Well, that isn't customary English is it? I made Hurree Singh say that. But, of course, I've expanded it a bit. I've never heard a Hindu say "The samefulness is terrific" …but you must make a thing entertaining.

Fisher T. Fish "was founded on an American 'drummer', what they call a commercial traveller. Fish does speak his own language, as spoken by other Americans. You make an American jump and he's quite likely to say, "Wake snakes!"

"Nobody ever wrote like I do, whether it's good, bad or indifferent. I'm quite individual. Solitary specimen. I know it sounds utterly absurd at my time of life, but when I'm sitting at a typewriter I'm only sixteen years old. Oh yes, I live at Greyfriars. Greyfriars

Denis Preston

School is a life of innocence. It's life as it should be. It's as things should be, and might be. And the more you impress that on the readers the more things are likely to be like that".

And there you have the philosophy of Charles Hamilton, in his own words, largely unknown until now. Thanks to Denis Preston's' enthusiasm and enterprise, we now have Hamilton's philosophy and where his famous characters came from in his own words.

Sir Arthur Conan Doyle

Sherlock Holmes Dr Watson Professor Challenger

How can it be that a fictional character can take on such stature and be so credible that tens of thousands believe that he is a real person, still miraculously alive? Created in 1887, aged about 40, Sherlock Holmes would have to be about 160 years old today. Yet readers from all over the world still write letters to him. That is the real mystery of Sherlock Holmes. The letters are sent to 221b Baker Street, where the Abbey National Building Society building stands today. Presumably, as a public relations exercise the Abbey National have an employee whose job it is to answer these letters to Sherlock Holmes. These are not children writing letters to Father Christmas at the North Pole, but adults of all nationalities and ages. They write to a Victorian consulting detective, who is deemed capable of helping them solve their problems today! The mind boggles.

Would it have made any difference if Sherlock Holmes' creator, Sir Arthur Conan Doyle, had stuck to the name he first thought of for his detective? Doyle's first choice was Ormond Sacker? Sherlock Holmes is certainly a better name. The whereabouts of the real 221b Baker Street has been for many years a matter of energetic debate and speculation. William Baring-gould, in his very comprehensive two volumes 'The Annotated Sherlock Holmes' goes to great lengths to pinpoint the exact site of Holmes' consulting rooms. When the first Sherlock Holmes story was published in 1881 Baker Street was not as long as it is now, starting at Portman Square and ending where it meets Crawford Street and Paddington Street. At this junction Baker Street became York Place. The street numbering system could not possibly have included a number as high as 221b. Experts W Baring-gould and Bernard Davies, have concluded that the present 31 Baker Street would have been a more likely site of the detectives world-famous address. The headquarters of Marks and Spencer now covers the site of number 31. Maybe M&S should be answering the letters!

Some twenty years ago I heard of a young man and his mother who were about to establish a Sherlock Holmes museum at a house they had purchased in Baker Street, not far from Regents Park. The Abbey National disapproved of this plan; probably because it would threaten their tenuous custodianship of the myth. Despite this, Sherlock Holmes museum was established, and I encouraged the enterprise. The house was exactly the right period and design. The rooms on the first floor were furnished, as accurately as possible, with artefacts mentioned in Conan Doyle's stories. The museum has become a mecca for Sherlock Holmes enthusiasts from all over the world. The museum provides a Meerschaum pipe and a deerstalker hat for visitors who wish to be photographed sitting in Holmes's famous basket chair. I once saw a Chinese lady tourist, so attired, posing for the camera.

A man dressed in the uniform of a Victorian policeman stands at the door keeping the Queen's peace. Inside, museum employees attired in the caps and aprons of Victorian housemaids assist the visitors. There is a basement shop selling books, pictures, ornaments, and videos. Sherlock Holmes is very much alive and thriving in this corner of London.

How did Conan Doyle 'discover' his immortal detective? In the first story, *A Study In Scarlet,* Holmes meets Dr. Watson for the first time in a laboratory in St. Bartholomew's Hospital. Here Watson is given the first example of Holmes's deductive and forensic powers. Dr. Watson describes the scene thus: "This was a lofty chamber, lined and littered with countless bottles. Broad low tables were scattered about, which bristled with retorts, test tubes, and little Bunsen lamps with their blue flickering flames. There was only one student in the room, who was bending over a distant table absorbed in his work. At the sound of our steps he glanced round and sprang to his feet with a cry of pleasure. "I found it! I found it," he shouted to my companion, running towards us with a test tube in his hand. "I found a Reagent, which is precipitated haemoglobin, and by nothing else." He had discovered a gold mine; greater delight could not have shone upon his features. "Dr. Watson, Mr. Sherlock Holmes", said Stamford, introducing us. "How are you?" he said cordially, gripping my hand with a strength for which I should hardly have given him credit. "You have been in Afghanistan, I perceive." "How on earth did you know that?" I asked in astonishment. "Never mind", he said, chuckling to himself. "The question now is about haemoglobin. No doubt, you see the significance of this discovery of mine?" "It is interesting, chemically, no doubt," I answered, "But practically ---" "Why, man, it is the most practical medico-legal discovery for years. Don't you see that it gives us an infallible test for bloodstains? Come over here now!" He seized me by the coat sleeve, in his eagerness, and drew me over to the table at which he had been working. "Let us have some fresh blood," he said, digging a long bodkin into his finger and drawing off the resulting drop of blood in a chemical pipette. "Now, I add this small quantity of blood to a litre of water. You perceive that the resulting mixture has the appearance of pure water. The proportion of blood cannot be more than one in a million. I have no doubt, however, that we shall be able to obtain the characteristic reaction". As he spoke, he threw into the vessel a few white crystals, and then added some drops of a transparent fluid. In an instant the contents assumed a dull mahogany colour and a brownish dust was precipitated to the bottom of the glass jar. "Ha! Ha!" he cried, clapping his hands, and looking as delighted as a child with a new toy. "What do you think of that?"

Compare this piece of Conan Doyle's fiction with his own recollections as a medical student at Edinburgh University. One of his professors was Dr. Joseph Bell, of whom Doyle writes: 'For some reason, which I have never understood, he singled me out from the drove of students who frequented his wards, and made me his out-patient clerk, which meant that I had to array his out-patients, make simple notes of their cases and then show them in, one by one, to the large room in which Dr. Bell sat in state, surrounded by his dressers and students. Then I had ample chance of studying his methods and of noticing that he often learned more of the patient by a few quick glances than I had done by my questions. Occasionally the results were very dramatic, though there were times when he blundered. In one of his best cases, he said to a civilian patient: "Well, my man, you've served in the army." "Aye, sir." "Not long discharged?" "No, sir." "A Highland regiment?" "Aye, sir." "A non-com officer?" "Aye, sir." "Stationed at Barbados?" "Aye, sir." "You see, gentlemen," he would explain, "the man was a respectful man but he did not remove his hat. They do not in the army, but he would have learned civilian ways had he been long discharged. He has an air of authority and he is obviously Scottish. As to Barbados, his complaint elephantiasis is West Indian and not British." To his audience of Watson's it all seemed very miraculous until it was explained, and then it became simple and easy enough. 'It is no wonder that after the study of such a character I used and amplified his methods when in later life I tried to build up a scientific detective, who solved cases on his own merits and not through the folly of the criminal. Bell took a keen interest in these detective tales and even made suggestions which were not, I am bound to say, very practical.'

As to the physical appearance of Dr. Bell he is described as having piercing grey eyes, an aquiline nose, a wiry body and a strident voice that demanded attention. Doyle described Holmes, on different occasions, as 'tall, thin, with sharp piercing grey eyes, a hawkish nose, and a strident voice'. The two descriptions make an interesting comparison.

The success of Doyle's greatest creation Sherlock Holmes was almost immediate when the first story *A Study In Scarlet* appeared in the *Strand Magazine*. This was followed by twelve stories under the title of *The Adventures of Sherlock Holmes*. Doyle was beginning to tire of the character whilst writing a further eleven new stories under the title of *The Memoirs of* Sherlock Holmes, and felt that he had nearly exhausted any new material for further stories; or at any rate would not be up to the standard he had established. So, he decided to 'kill off' Holmes.

In December 1893, Doyle and his wife were on holiday in Switzerland. It occurred to him that the dramatic Reichenbach Falls would be the ideal location to play out the final confrontation between Holmes and his archenemy Professor Moriarty. He had them in a 'to the death' struggle overlooking the falls, before carrying each other over the edge and into the mist filled ravine below. Presumed drowned. Doyle wrote to a friend, at the time: 'I couldn't revive him if I would, at least not for years, for I have had such an overdose of him that I feel towards him as I do towards pate de fois gras, of which I once ate too much, so that the name of it gives me a sickly feeling to this day.' So that the thought of his famous hero, by then, made him feel sick! But the public were far from happy at being denied the stories to which they had become addicted. Some implored him, some even sent threatening letters. Doyle resisted the clamber until 1902, when his finances needed a boost.

Dartmoor is sometimes described as the last wilderness in Britain. Folklore abounds there and has done so for centuries. It was whilst staying with a friend, Fletcher Robinson, in Devon that the foundations for a new book were laid. It would turn out to be his most famous and possibly most popular story – *The Hound of the Baskervilles*. Fletcher Robinson had a coachman called Harry Baskerville and that is where Doyle found the name. Whilst staying on Dartmoor, he heard of folklore concerning phantom hounds on the Moors, the hounds of hell? Hound Tor is the site of a medieval village and their ruins woven into the story, Holmes hides out amongst them. Lew House is most likely to be the original for 'Baskerville Hall'. It matches up to the aspects mentioned in the book. Doyle stayed there and its atmosphere influenced him in weaving the great mystery adventure. The village of Grimpen is thought to be 'Widdecombe-in-the-moor'. The deadly Grimpen Mire is nearby. Doyle must have greatly appreciated the help given to him by Fletcher Robinson, for he dedicated the book to him.

Sherlock Holmes was back in business in a big way. Doyle followed *The Hound of the Baskervilles* with further stories in *The Return of* Sherlock Holmes.

Dr Joseph Bell

Sherlock Holmes

Glowing hound, as illustrated by Sidney Paget for the *Strand Magazine*

Lew Hall

Professor Challenger

Doyle, whilst a medical student, also took the physical characteristics and temperament from another of his Professors, John Rutherford, the anatomist, whom, he described as an eccentric man with a dark beard, and bellowing voice. Doyle was to use him as the example on which to base the character of the overbearing Professor Challenger in *The Lost World.*

An interesting piece of information is that Robert Louis Stevenson was a great admirer of Doyle, who in turn had been a great influence on Doyle's' early writing. An unanswered question: Was major Alfred Wood, Doyle's secretary for forty years, Dr. Watson? Some have said so.

Basil Rathbone, the definitive Sherlock Holmes on film

So we might end this chapter with what could have been a typical exchange between Holmes and Watson. Watson: "So, you mean Holmes, that..."

Holmes: "Exactly that!"

Watson: "... that Dr. Joseph Bell, of Edinburgh University was the consulting detective – extraordinary!"

Holmes: "Elementary, my dear Watson, elementary!"

Photograph of the Baker Street set built at Pinewood Studios, for Billy Wilder's film: *The Private Life of Sherlock Holmes*

Kenneth Grahame

Mr Toad

The Wind In The Willows is commonly regarded as a charming book for children about the cosy lives of animals with human attributes. The book is enriched by beautiful and poetic descriptions of the English countryside in all its seasons. On another level, the book can also be read as an allegory of its time, and from the standpoint of which it was written — an emotional and rather apprehensive writers' observations of the social upheaval he was either witnessing or anticipating.

Remarkably, Kenneth Grahame cannot really be thought of as a 'professional writer'. Apart from *The Wind In The Willows*, his output was rather small and relatively unremarkable. He spent most of his time in banking, rising eventually to become the Secretary of the Bank of England, which couldn't really be considered a 'part time' or a 'fill in' job for a busy productive writer like Stevenson or Dickens.

Born in Scotland in 1859, Grahame had an unsettled childhood. His mother died when he was five, and his father, a heavy drinker, was incapable of caring for the children, three boys and a girl, who were sent to live with their maternal grandmother in Cookham Dean, Berkshire. It is here that Grahame's lifelong love of boating and the English countryside was born. The spell of the river would remain with him all his life. Young Kenneth was shunted around to relations in different places; at the age of eight he was sent to St Edwards Boarding School in Oxford, where, in spite of the spartan regime and the inexplicable coldness of the headmaster, Grahame eventually became head boy.

As a young man he yearned for a stable relationship. He was shy. He got a job as a junior clerk at the Bank of England through family connections, which wouldn't have left much time for any writing. In 1895 the publisher, John Lane, at Bodley Head, agreed to publish his collection of articles brought together under the title of *The Golden Age*. Lane was also the publisher of the notorious *Yellow Book*, the monthly publication associated with the Aesthetic Movement – William Morris, Oscar Wilde, and the artist Aubrey Beardsley. Grahame was invited to contribute to the publication. He was flattered and felt drawn to the rebellious ethos of the aesthetes. He remained, however, a true innocent and was shocked, along with most of English society, by the revelations of the Oscar Wilde trials. They were a body blow to the *Yellow Book* and the Aesthetic Movement. Grahame sought to remove himself from the company of the group to concentrate his energies on his job at the bank. During his time at the bank, over the fifteen years before becoming its secretary in 1898, he had hoped that he might find the confidence to become a full time professional writer, but he never found the courage to do so. He felt he had never grown up emotionally and never felt happier or safer than in the realms of fantasy and childhood. In this way he was much like J M Barrie, Edward Lear, and Lewis Carroll. He found a degree of emotional stability in his marriage to Elspeth Thomson, who shared his sentimental love of all things childish. She genuinely loved him and hoped that he would be able to reciprocate her feelings to the same degree, but he found this difficult; they would converse and write to each other in their own childlike language.

Much of Kenneth Grahame's spare time was devoted to his passion for boating. "Messing about in boats", (says the Water Rat says in *The Wind In The Willows*) "Believe me, my young friend, there is *nothing* – absolutely nothing – half so much worth doing as simply messing about in boats". It has been suggested that a close friend, Edward Atkinson, 'Atky', who was the Commodore of the Fowey Yacht Club in Cornwall, was the original for the character of the Water Rat – 'Ratty'.

In 1900 the Grahame's child Alistair was born. When the boy was four years old Grahame started to tell him bits of stories about a toad, but it was not until 1907 that all his pent up emotions came tumbling out in *The Wind In The Willows*. Alistair suffered from physical disabilities after his premature birth, suffered a congenital cataract in his sightless right eye together with a pronounced squint affecting his left eye; in addition he was not over bright, although his snobbish mother thought otherwise and remained certain that the boy was destined to reach great academic heights. "A brilliant boy", she said, despite of the total absence of any evidence supporting such optimism. She dominated the boy and influenced him in every respect. She even dressed him in girlish clothes. Alistair became chronically spoilt; he developed a precocious vocabulary. One twelve-year-old child said to him "You're only a boy who swallowed a dictionary!" He was headstrong and given to emotional outbursts, not helped by the pressure of his mother's high-flown expectations.

On a family holiday in Scotland, Grahame was overheard telling Alistair a bedtime story – the toad had now been joined by a mole, a water rat and a badger. Thus the story was taking shape. It had started as mainly about Mr Toad. The chapters concerning him were written first; the two very different chapters, *The Piper*

The Riverbank, as painted by Arthur Rackham

Toad being dressed as a washerwoman, enabling him to escape from prison. Painted by Arthur Rackham.

At The Gates and *Wayfarers All*, were added later. These were separate from the central thrust of a child's story, reaching new emotional heights and containing some of the most beautiful descriptive passages in the book about the English countryside.

In *The Piper At The Gates* the mole and the water rat had been rowing all night on the river, in search of a lost baby otter. The heat of the summer night is subsiding and a cooler new day is breaking.

'*On either side of them, as they glided onwards, the rich meadow-grass seemed that morning of a freshness and greenness unsurpassable. Never had they noticed the roses so vivid, the willow-herb so riotous, the meadow-sweet so odorous and pervading. Then the murmur of the approaching weir began to the hold the air, and they felt a consciousness that they were nearing the end, whatever it might be, that surely awaited their expedition.*

A wide half-circle of foam and glinting lights and shining shoulders of green water, the great weir closed the backwater from bank to bank, troubled all the quiet surface with twirling eddies and floating foam-streaks, and deadened all other sounds with its solemn and soothing rumble. In the midmost of the stream, embraced in the weirs shimmering arms-spread a small island lay anchored, fringed close with willow and silver birch and alder. Reserved, shy, but full of significance, it hid whatever it might hold behind a veil, keeping it till the hour should come, and with the hour, those who were called and chosen.'

In *Wayfarers All*: '*Restlessly the rat wandered off once more, climbed the slope that rose gently from the north bank of the river, and lay looking out towards the great ring of downs that barred his vision further southwards – his simple horizon hitherto, his mountains of the moon, his limit behind which lay nothing he had cared to see or know. Today, to him gazing south with a newborn need stirring in his heart, the clear sky over the long low outline seemed to pulsate with promise; today, the unseen was everything, the unknown the only real fact of life. On this side of the hills was now a real blank, on the other lay the clouded and coloured panorama that his inner eye was seeing so clearly. What seas lay beyond, green, leaping, and crested! What sunbathed coasts along which the white villas glittered against the olive woods! What quiet harbours, thronged with gallant shipping bound for purple islands of wine and spice, islands set low in languorous waters*!'

The contrast in depth of these chapters is remarkable.

Much of Alistair's tantrums and outbursts 'kicking and wailing' Grahame transferred into Toad's childishness. In the chapter Toad's Adventures, Badger appears as a father figure, remonstrating with a rebellious child: ' *"No!" he said a little sullenly, but stoutly; "I'm not sorry. And it wasn't folly at all! It was simply glorious! "What?!" cried the Badger, greatly scandalised. "You backsliding animal, didn't you tell me just now, in there – ' 'O, yes, yes, in there. You're so eloquent, dear Badger, and so moving, and so convincing, and put all your points so frightfully well – you can do what you like with me in there, and you know it. But I've been searching my mind since, and going over things in it, and I find that I'm not a bit sorry or repentant really, so it's no earthly good saying I am; now is it?" "Then you don't promise," said the Badger, "never to touch a motor-car again?" "Certainly not!" replied* Toad *emphatically. "On the contrary, I faithfully promise that the very first motor-car I see, poop-poop! Off I go in it!" "Told you so, didn't I?" observed the Rat to the Mole. "Very well, then," said the Badger firmly, rising to his feet. "Since you won't yield to persuasion, we'll try what force can do. I feared it would come to this all along. You've often asked us three to come and stay with you,* Toad, *in this handsome house of yours; well, now we're going to. When we've converted you to a proper point of view we may quit, but not before. Take him upstairs, you two, and lock him up in his bedroom, while we arrange matters between ourselves." "It's for your own good,* Toady, *you know," said the Rat kindly, as* Toad, *kicking and struggling, was hauled up the stairs by his two faithful friends.*'

For Toad's bombast and boasting Grahame drew on the personality of an infamous politician of the day – Horatio Bottomley, a recently elected and remarkably popular Socialist MP. Later he was exposed as a flamboyant fraudster who had embezzled large amounts of money by shady deals on the stock exchange. After living in the lap of luxury for ten years he was questioned about the whereabouts of a missing sum of seven hundred thousand pounds. He disarmingly replied, "In all sincerity and honesty, gentlemen, I do not know what has become of the money". In 1922, he was sentenced to seven years penal servitude. Toad went to jail, but Mr Toad was no embezzler.

Kenneth Grahame put all his anxieties and apprehensions about social change and unrest into his story, as well as his nostalgic longing for an idealised, pre-industrial, agricultural, essentially aristocratic society. Grahame feared the looming shadows of an increasingly uncertain age, creating the Wild Wooders – Stoats and Weasels, the newly emerging socialists, who were threatening the peaceful old order. All these fears are implied in what purports to be a simple tale for children.

The Wind In The Willows was a great popular success, and Grahame tried to arouse the interest of theatre managers with a view to producing it on stage. They all turned it down on the grounds that it was 'too fey'. However, A A Milne, creator of *Winnie-the-Pooh*, was quick to recognise its stage potential and offered to transform the book into a stage play for children to be titled: *Toad of Toad Hall*. Produced for the first time in 1930, it is regularly re-staged as a Christmas show for children, rivalling popularity of pantomime. There are, of course, elements of pantomime purposefully included in the play.

The original book illustrations for *The Wind In The Willows* were by E H Shepard. After Grahame's death his widow led Arthur Rackham to the places identified by Grahame in the story. Rackham was commissioned to paint a new collection of illustrations.

Here, I include a couple of personal reminisces about *The Wind In The Willows.*

In the first-ever production of the play the role of Mole was performed by Richard Goolden, who thereafter made the part his own, playing it for forty years until his death in the Seventies. He acted in many other plays and films, and was a regular performer on radio. I cast him in a revival of our musical *Lock Up Your Daughters* because, apart from his being right for the role, I confess that I was eager to meet this link with the first *Toad of Toad Hall.* I learned that Richard Goolden had actually

Alistair Grahame

Horatio Bottomley

Mr Toad,
as illustrated by E.H. Shepherd

worked as a clerk at the Bank of England, under Kenneth Grahame! He said that Grahame had always been very kind and courteous to his juniors. Richard Goolden regularly sent me Christmas cards, personally illustrated for each recipient.

Christmas card from actor, Richard Goolden (the original 'mole') in *Toad of Toad Hall*

My deep affection and respect for *The Wind In The Willows* led me to initiate an unabridged audio recording of the book, which was beautifully read by David Davis, one time head of BBC radio's celebrated *Children's Hour*. I produced this with Nigel and Gillian Brandt of Unicorn/Kanchana Records; gratifyingly, it won the Gramophone Industry Award for 1982. The incidental music I composed for this recording I later turned into a tone poem for orchestra.

There is a sad post-script to this chapter. Alistair Grahame eventually succumbed to the pressure of his mother's expectations and enrolled as an undergraduate at Oxford. One night he lay on a rail track in the path of a train, and was decapitated. Poor Mr Toad.

A.A. Milne

Christopher Robin

A Milne was born in 1882 in Hampstead, and had a very happy childhood. He attended his father's school where the writer H.G. Wells was, for some time, his teacher. Milne was a successful playwright and author before *Winnie-the-Pooh* ever entered his head. He had written a very popular comedy called *Mr Pim Passes By*, also *Other People's Lives* and *The Dover Road*. But, like J M Barrie, creator of Peter Pan, Milne would eventually be remembered for his classic books for children rather than anything else they had written. Milne hoped one day to write what he called a 'powerful novel'. He could not have imagined that the bedtime stories he had concocted for his son, about his toy bear, would prove to be more 'powerful' than any novel he might have written.

In 1920 Milne's wife, Dorothy de Selincourt, who he called Daphne, gave birth to a baby boy. They named him Christopher Robin. His father chose the initials 'C R' because they would sound well as the name of a future great cricketer – C R Milne. He saw Christopher as a vehicle through which he could overcome his own disappointments. For the first five years of his life Christopher was brought up mainly by his nurse, Olive Rand, later to be immortalised as Alice (so as to rhyme with 'Palace') in a famous poem: 'They're changing guard at Buckingham Palace, Christopher Robin went down with Alice'. It was the custom, in upper middle class families in the twenties, for children to be the principal responsibility of the nurse who would come down from the nursery, with her small charges, to see the parents at particular times, or on special occasions.

Christopher, looking back to these childhood years, wrote: 'If I cannot say that I loved my parents, it is only, because, in those early days I just didn't know them well enough'. He also made a significant comment on Milne's character: 'Some people are good with children, others are not. It is a gift, you either have it or you don't. My father didn't.' A A Milne himself said: 'I'm not inordinately fond of, or interested in, children. I have never felt in the least sentimental about them.'

Christopher Robin's nickname at home was Billy, though he was later known as Moon (from his own mispronunciation of Milne). Alan and Daphne were preoccupied with their own separate interests, she with gardening, and he with golf. They had no shared interests, but, to quote Milne: 'She always laughed at my jokes'. The arrival of a baby had upset their well-ordered routines. But, thanks to nurse Olive Rand, they were able to continue to live their lives much as before.

A A Milne, Christopher Robin with *Winnie-the-Pooh*

They didn't have Christopher's hair cut for a long time. People mistook Christopher and said: "Oh, what a pretty little girl." The long hair reminded Daphne of the little girl she'd always wanted. She dressed him in girlish clothes… 'smocks and things' Christopher recalled in later life, adding: 'In my very earliest dreams I even used to dream that I was a girl'. He loved Alice very much and she was devoted to him. She even delayed marrying her fiancé for some years until Christopher Robin no longer needed her.

In 1923 Milne made a present of his poem *Vespers* to Daphne. This was to become better known as *Christopher Robin Is Saying His Prayers*. Milne said she could get it published if she wished and keep the royalties. She did so and it was an immediate success.

The following years, living mostly in the country at Cotchford Farm, Sussex, Milne wrote *When We Were Very Young*, the collection of poems (*The Kings Breakfast*, *Nursery Chairs Jonathan Jo*, etc.) When published in America, letters of appreciation flooded in from all sorts of people, from President Coolidge to Fred Astaire. Everyone in the U.S., it seems, was quoting A A Milne. *The Sunday Herald Post* ran a family photograph with the caption: 'A A Milne, and his wife and *little girl*.' H Fraser-Simson, who had written the popular musical *The Maid of the Mountain*s, set fourteen of Milne's rhymes to music.

Winnie was an American black bear Christopher often visited at London Zoo, and the *Pooh* was Christopher Robin's own invention. Christopher's toy bear was called Edward, as many bears are, but Milne thought that he should have 'an exciting name' all to himself. Immediately Christopher Robin said "*Winnie-the-Pooh*", and from that moment that's exactly who he was. When Milne started to write the book, in January 1926, he immediately brought other toys in the nursery, Eeyore and Piglet, into the story. He invented Owl and Rabbit. He started writing at a great pace, the stories coming easily to him. Daphne bought Kanga and Roo at Harrods, and they came into the stories. By March the book was nearly complete. When E H Shepard, the artist, came to start drawing the characters he said he used his own son, Graham, as the model for Christopher Robin, whose own legs were considered too skinny. But, Christopher Robin later insisted that he was the true model, and that the drawings looked just like him.

Whilst Milne read the stories aloud Christopher Robin would play with the animal characters on the floor. At the same time E H Shepard would make sketches for the illustrations, which would go into the book. But at the time Christopher was unaware that he was the inspiration for both the writer and the illustrator. Christopher acts as a father to the animals in the stories and we all know people with the personalities that Milne gave to the animals. Milne dedicated the book to Daphne :

You gave me Christopher Robin, and then
You breathed new life in Pooh.
Whatever of each has left my pen
Goes homing back to you.
My book is ready, and comes to greet
The mother it longs to see –
It would be my present to you, my sweet,
If it weren't your gift to me.

A further book of poems, *Now We Are Six*, followed. Milne was writing inspired by returning to his own boyhood and in Christopher he found the companion with whom he could return there. But being known as Christopher Robin of the Pooh books became a tiresome burden for him as he was growing up. With the onset of war in 1939 he gained anonymity as an officer in the Royal Engineers where he distinguished himself in action. He married in 1948 and enjoyed a happy and rewarding life running a bookshop in Dartmouth.

In his autobiography *Enchanted Places* Christopher Robin's last comment on his father was: 'My father's heart remained buttoned up all through his life and I wouldn't attempt to unbutton it, to write about the things he never spoke about.' Christopher Robin Milne died in 1996.

A sad postscript: Pop musician Brian Jones purchased the Milne's family home, Cotchford Farm, in 1968 and tragically died in the swimming pool there a year later.

The original Eeyore, Winnie-the-Pooh, Piglet, Tigger and Kanga

The original Winnie-the-Pooh

W.S. Gilbert

Sir Joseph Porter The Three Aesthetes

William Schwenck Gilbert was born in London in 1836, the year Queen Victoria came to the throne. The great lyric writer, Ira Gershwin, said that Gilbert was the first real lyricist. Gilbert himself liked to be known as a 'dramatist', which covered his many talents including that of a librettist. In fact, he ensured that the word 'dramatist' was carved on his headstone. With the composer, Arthur Sullivan, born in Lambeth in 1842, Gilbert became half of the unique partnership of Gilbert and Sullivan who, between them, created the great legacy of the fourteen D'oyly Carte operas. Richard D'oyly Carte was a remarkable man and an essential part of the triumvirate. He financed and guided the ventures. In addition, he built 'The Palace', 'The Garrick' and 'The

Savoy' theatres, also The Savoy Hotel, in which Gilbert and Sullivan were shareholders.

One of the earliest great successes was 'HMS Pinafore'. W S Gilbert was very amused by the appointment of the Prime Minister, Benjamin Disraeli, of W H Smith, the publisher and founder of the famous newsagent chain, as first Lord of the Admiralty. What Gilbert found most amusing and which he parodied with the character of Sir Joseph Porter was the fact that the first Lord of the Admiralty had never been to sea.

The song lyric charts the rise of the fictitious character Sir Joseph Porter.

When I was a lad I served my term
As office boy to an Attorney's firm.
I cleaned the windows and I swept the floor,
And I polished up the handle of the big front door.
I polished up that handle so carefullee
That now I am the Ruler of the Queen's Navee!

As office boy I made such a mark
That they gave me the post of a junior clerk.
I served the writs with a smile so bland.
And I copied all the letters in a big round hand –
I copied all the letters in a hand so free,
That now I am the Ruler of the Queen's Navee!

In serving writs I made such a name
That an articled clerk I soon became;
I wore clean collars and a brand new suit
For the pass examination at the Institute.
And that pass examination did so well for me,
That now I am the Ruler of the Queen's Navee!

Of legal knowledge I acquired such a grip
That they took me into the partnership.
And that junior partnership I ween
Was the only ship I had ever seen.

But that kind of ship so suited me,
That now I am the Ruler of the Queen's Navee!

I grew so rich that I was sent
By a pocket borough into Parliament.
I always voted at my party's call,
And I never thought of thinking for myself at all.
I thought so little they rewarded me,
By making me the Ruler of the Queen's Navee!

Now landsmen all, whoever you may be,
If you want to rise to the top of the tree,
If your soul isn't fettered to an office stool,
Be careful to be guided by this golden rule –
Stick close to your desks and never go to sea,
And you all may be Rulers of the Queen's Navee!

Gilbert's favourites among his own operas appear to have been the *The Mikado* and *Patience.* He seems to have been searching for a somewhat unusual or even sensational basis for the story of *Patience.* He had considered various ideas; one concerned two comic curates, who attracted a couple of lady parishioners. One of the curates was known as 'the Reverend Lawntennison!' But Gilbert got cold feet and abandoned the project, fearing the wrath of the Church of England. Then he considered another idea concerning the ritual and vestments of the Anglo-Catholic Church, but he dropped this for the same reason.

The Aesthetic Movement was becoming popular around 1881, led principally by William Morris, the painter James Whistler, Oscar Wilde, and the poet Algernon

Sir Arthur Sullivan

Richard D'Oyly Carte

Swinburne. London was experiencing a fashion fad, which saw men wearing affected dress, and displaying affected manners and gestures; we would call it 'camp' today. In the programme for *Patience* D'Oyly Carte wrote mockingly of: "the outpourings of a clique of professors of ultra refinement who preach the gospel of morbid languor and sickly sensuousness, which is half real and half affected by its high priests for the purpose of gaining social notoriety" (sounds familiar today). "The authors of *Patience* have not desired to cast ridicule on the true aesthetic spirit, but only to attack the unmanly oddities which masquerade in its likeness".

Unmanly oddities! Gilbert chose three of these as his models for *Patience*: Oscar

Wilde, James McNeil Whistler and Algernon Swinburne for the three Aesthetes in the opera. They were attired in gay velvet jackets, knee britches and floppy tam-o-shanter-like bonnets. Leading this trio of colourful gents was the star of the operas, George Grossmith as the character Reginald Bunthorne, 'camped it up' to the delight of packed houses. Oscar Wilde had heard that he, along with Whistler and Swinburne, was being parodied and he was intrigued enough to write to George Grossmith requesting a box for the first night. Gilbert decided to make composite characters out of the three but ended up with Bunthorne having the lions share of 'Wilde'.

Typical of Gilbert's jaunty style of lyrics in the excerpt from Patience:

<u>The Aesthete</u>
If you're anxious for to shine
In the high aesthetic line
As a man of culture rare
You must get up all the germs
Of the transcendental terms
And plant them everywhere
You must lie upon the daisies
And discourse in novel phrases
Of your complicated state of mind
The meaning doesn't matter
If its only idle chatter
Of a transcendental kind

And everyone will say as you walk your mystique way

"If this young man expresses himself in terms too deep for me
Why, what a very singularly deep young man
This deep young man must be."

Be eloquent in praise
Of the very dull old days
Which have long since passed away
And convince 'em, if you can
That the reign of good Queen Anne
Was culture's palmiest day
Of course you pooh-pooh
Whatever's fresh and new
And declare it's crude and mean
And that Art stopped short
In the cultivated court
Of the Empress Josephine
And everyone will say as you walk your mystique way

"If that's not good enough for him which is good enough for me
Why, what a very cultivated kind of youth
This kind of youth must be."

Then a sentimental passion
Of a vegetable fashion
Must excite your languid spleen
An attachment *a la* Plato
For a bashful young potato
Or a not-too-french-french-bean!
Though the Philistines may jostle
You will rank as an apostle
In the high aesthetic band
If you walk down Piccadilly
With a poppy or a lily
In your medieval hand

And everyone will say as you walk your flowr'y way

"If he's content with a vegetable love which would certainly not suit me
Why, what a most particularly pure young man
This pure young man must be!"

Patience was well received. The Daily News reported 'The composer's settings of the lyrical portions of Mr Gilbert's witty satire are in nearly every case, bright and melodious. The sentiment and grace of most of Mr Sullivan's music gives the additional zest to the quaintness and humour of the other portions, and there can be little doubt that these qualities and merits of Mr Gilbert's book will secure a success as great as any that hitherto resulted from the same cooperation'.

Oscar Wilde

It is not known what the young Oscar Wilde really felt or said after seeing the opera, but according to Hesketh Pearson in his book The Life of Oscar Wilde he writes 'Gilbert, who was clever enough to spot that Wilde, like Bunthorne, had "more innocent fun within me than a casual spectator would imagine", and was enjoying his own performance while chuckling at the spectators. Wilde justified Gilbert's opinion of him by laughing heartedly at *Patience*'. The very astute D'oyly Carte arranged for Wilde to go on a lucrative lecture tour of America, through Carte's own agency, which ensured that Wilde would appear in each city at the same time as *Patience* opened there. On one occasion in Omaha the local newspaper reported 'He wore a suit of black velvet with knee britches which had been his usual dress in this country. His hair fell about his shoulders in heavy masses, his dreamy poetic face grew animated, and his large dark eyes lighted up as he entered upon his subject.'

The Three Aesthetes from *Patience*

Patience opened in London at The Opera Comique and transferred to Carte's new theatre The Savoy, which boasted 'the new electric light'. Enterprisingly, Carte appeared on stage holding an electric light. As *The Electrical Times* reported 'A hush fell upon the audience, who thought that electricity was always fatal. He then delighted, with a sort of, polytechnic lecture ... respecting the safety with electric light to the theatre. Finally, he placed a piece of muslin round the lamp and held it up ... he then took a hammer and smashed the lamp that, naturally, went out. But when he held up the muslin, unburned, the affect on the audience was electric, in both senses of the word. D'oyly Carte bowed himself off amidst enthusiastic cheers, which were so prolonged that he had to go on and take two calls.

Amongst my grandfather's music books, of which I have one, dated 1883, I found a lyric describing the dramatic impact of the arrival of electricity in London's theatreland.

The New Electric Light
(The Song of the Times)
Chorus
Our cousins from the country are astonished at the sight
The little stars are striking, and the gas it won't burn bright;
The moon has got the 'vapours', while the lime-light's taken fright
All through that big sensation, the new electric light.

The new electric light wasn't the only thing that was illuminating the audiences of *Patience*. The Oscar Wilde trials must have thrown a different light on the Aesthetic Movement, which went into hiding and faded away when other aspects hitherto unknown to the polite public came to light.

A personal footnote: My great-great uncle owned a Georgian town-house in the corner of Soho Square. My great aunt Melita sometimes stayed there as a little girl and remembering watching from an upstairs window while an organ grinder and his traditional monkey performed in the square below. This would have been around the mid 1870's. Thomas Blackwell, of the famous grocers Crosse and Blackwell later acquired the house. It became, first, his home and subsequently the HQ of the company. The house boasted a spiral staircase rising from the entrance hall through four floors to a large glass domed skylight in the roof. I, recently, popped into the building and am glad to report that the beautiful staircase still stands. Thomas Blackwell also bought a country house 'The Cedars' in Harrow Weald, where his neighbour was none other than W S Gilbert.

Grim's Dyke – last home of W S Gilbert

Oscar Wilde

James McNeil Whistler

Algernon Swinburne

PATIENCE

Bunthorne's Bride — Æsthetic Opera

W. S. GILBERT · ARTHUR SULLIVAN

CHORUS OF OFFICERS OF DRAGOON GUARDS.

The Lady Angela,	Rapturous Maidens	Miss Jessie Bond.
The Lady Saphir,		Miss Julia Gwynne.
The Lady Ella,		Miss Fortescue.
The Lady Jane,		Miss Alice Barnett.
Patience, a Dairymaid,		Miss Leonora Braham.

CHORUS OF RAPTUROUS MAIDENS.

Act 1.—Exterior of Castle Bunthorne. Act 2.—A Glade.

Musical Conductor—Mr. FRANK CELLIER. Stage Manager—Mr. W. H. SEYMOUR.

MOCK TURTLES

NO FEES OF ANY KIND

Original programme of *Patience*

My aunt Melita, looking out of the window into Soho Square, would also have seen a granite statue of Charles II (1681), which in the 1890's was becoming in need of repair. Since the local residents were unwilling to pay for the statue's restoration, Blackwell was asked if he could find a friend on whom the statue could be unloaded. Blackwell offered it to Gilbert, who agreed to have it. The statue was duly delivered to Grim's Dyke – very close to where I live today - and after restoration was placed on a small island in the middle of the lake that Gilbert had constructed. Sadly, this was to be the place where he died of a heart attack whilst bathing in 1911. In 1936, Lady Gilbert, when moving from Grim's Dyke made a gift of the statue to Soho Square, where it still stands today. Gilbert had said that when he died he wished it could be in his own garden on a summer's day. Ironically, his wish was granted.

Sir William Gilbert writing in the library of Grim's Dyke

Charles Dickens Gallery

David Copperfield	Mr & Mrs Micawber	Wackford Squeers
Dora Spenlow	Flora Finching	Little Nell
Ebenezer Scrooge	Estella	Miss Havisham

Charles Dickens was born in 1812 in Portsea. Throughout his life he drew his fictional characters from real life, and real situations. Sometimes he would 'borrow' no more than an amusing or unusual name. For his novel 'Oliver Twist' he recalled he had seen above a shop front. The name of an old school friend Bob 'Fagin'. Anything and everybody was fair game to Charles Dickens. He was an astute observer of human nature, and eccentric characters; his uncanny ear for dialogue still seems amusing and convincing today.

David Copperfield and Mr & Mrs Micawber

Dickens's early life is reflected in David Copperfield where he was able to relive the emotional ups and downs of his youth. 'D.C.- C.D'! His father, John Dickens, became Mr Micawber with all his optimism, a loving father, always trying to make ends meet. He was a pay clerk in the dockyard at Chatham.

When the family moved to London, with the hope that the financial situation might improve the opposite happened. Charles had to be put to work in a blacking factory, where his job was to put boot blacking into little jars and tie paper lids to them. His experience in Warren's Blacking Factory was transformed into Murdstone & Grinby's bottle washing factory in David Copperfield. All the degradation and loneliness that Charles felt at this time is clearly depicted in the novel. He felt bitterly ashamed of the situation in which he found himself and, forever after, felt himself unable to walk down that particular side of the street, near Hungerford Bridge, where the Blacking Factory was situated.

Whilst the young David Copperfield was toiling in the bottle-washing factory it became necessary for him to go into lodgings with the Micawber family. Mrs Micawber, who was based upon Charles's mother, opens her heart to the young David, "I never thought" said Mrs Micawber; when she came up, twins and all, to show me the apartment, and sat down to take a breath, "before I was married, when I lived with Papa and Mama, that I should ever find it necessary to take a lodger. But Mr Micawber being in difficulties, all considerations of private feelings must give way. Mr Micawber's difficulties are almost overwhelming just at present and whether it is possible to bring him through them, I don't know. When I lived at home with Papa and Mama, I really should have hardly understood what the word meant, in the sense in which I now employ it, but it experentia does it – as Papa used to say. If Mr Micawber's creditors *will not* give him time, they must take the consequences; and the sooner they bring it to an issue the better. Blood cannot be obtained from a stone neither can anything on account be obtained at present (not to mention law

Charles Dickens

expenses) from Mr Micawber.' Mr Micawber's creditors did indeed bring things to an issue, which resulted in his being committed to the Marshalsea Debtor's Prison.

John Dickens was eventually sentenced in the Marshalsea Debtor's Prison for non-payment of bills. This was a very grim place. Mr Micawber was likewise held there, and Charles's boyhood memories of the Marshalsea are described in depressing detail. 'Mr Micawber was waiting for me within the gate, and we went up to his room (top storey but one), and cried very much. He solemnly conjured me, I remember, to take warning by his fate; and to observe that if a man had twenty pounds a-year for his income, and spent nineteen pounds, nineteen shillings and sixpence, he would be happy, but if he spent twenty pounds *one* he would be miserable. After which he borrowed a shilling from me for porter, gave me a written order on Mrs Micawber, for the amount, and put away his pocket-handkerchief, and cheered up.'

I am presented to Mrs Micawber. [from *David Copperfield*; illustrator Fred Barnard]

When John Dickens was released from the Marshalsea, thanks to a relation coming to his financial assistance, in order to try and help the situation, his mother established a school for young ladies at their home in Gower Street, but that didn't work out because nobody came! Like her husband, she was the eternal optimist and supported her husband's efforts to gain suitable employment.

Charles Dickens's mother possessed the loyal qualities of Mrs Micawber and she was just as dotty as she was painted. In *David Copperfield* Dickens wrote: 'Poor Mrs Micawber! She said she had tried to excerpt herself; and so, I have no doubt, she had. The centre of the street door was perfectly covered with a great brass-plate, on which was engraved "Mrs Micawber's Boarding Establishment For Young Ladies"; but I never found that any young lady had ever been to school there; or that any young lady ever came, or proposed to come, or that the least preparation was ever made to receive any young lady. The only visitors I ever saw, or heard of, were creditors.

John Dickens

Micawber
[from *David Copperfield*; illustrator 'Phiz']

They used to come at all hours, and some of them were quite ferocious.'

Charles Dickens's recalls his early life with his mother and father in the dramatic exchanges of Mr and Mrs Micawber in their circumstances. Consider, for instance, Mrs Micawber's hysterical outburst "I will never desert Mr Micawber. Mr Micawber may have concealed his difficulties from me in the first instance, and his sanguine temper may have led him to expect that he would overcome them… but I never will desert Mr Micawber. No!" cried Mrs Micawber, more affected than before, "I never will do it! It's of no use asking me!" "I felt quite uncomfortable", observes young Copperfield, as if Mrs Micawber supposed I had asked her to do anything of the sort! - and sat looking at her in alarm. "Mr Micawber has his faults. I do not deny that he is improvident. I do not deny that he has kept me in the dark as to his resources and his liabilities both", she went on, looking at the wall; "But I will never desert Mr Micawber!" "Emma, my angel!" cried Mr Micawber, running into the room; "What is the matter?" "I never will desert you, Micawber!" she exclaimed. "My life!" said Mr Micawber, taking her in his arms. "I am perfectly aware of it." "He is the parent of my children! He is the father of my twins! He is the husband of my affections," cried Mrs Micawber, struggling; "and I ne-ver-will-desert Mr Micawber!"' Thus Charles Dickens, recalling the dramatic and emotional atmosphere of his early home life, shows the parallels in the family experiences of the young Copperfield and the young Dickens.

Wackford Squeers

Wackford Squeers sketched by 'Phiz' following his visit with Dickens to William Shaw's Bowes Academy

Charles was enrolled at the grandly titled Wellington House Academy, a seedy rundown private school in Camden Town, situated near where the Dickens family were then living. The school was run by a Mr Jones, who became Mr Creakle, the headmaster of the school that David Copperfield attended. All Charles's experiences can be read, clearly depicted, in his accounts of the second rate rundown school where the boys were so exploited, where "as much as possible was taken out of the boys and as little as possible put into them". When he was a grown man, and writing *Nicholas Nickleby,* Charles took care to condemn to expose awful schools such as those he had experienced.

One dreadful establishment, run by a one-eyed William Shaw, typified the scandalous state of some Yorkshire schools. The one-eyed man got his just desserts when Charles created one of his most famous grotesques in the character of the one-eyed Wackford Squeers in *Nicholas Nickleby.* Dickens, accompanied by the illustrator Hablot Browne ('Phiz'), did indeed visit William Shaw's school incognito and saw for himself the dreadful exploitation of children there.

Dickens describes the obnoxious headmaster thus: 'Mr Squeers' appearance was not prepossessing. He had but one eye, and the popular prejudice runs in favour of two. The eye he had was unquestionably useful, but decidedly not ornamental, being of a greenish grey, and in shape resembling a fanlight of a street door. The blank side of his face was wrinkled and puckered up, which gave him a very sinister appearance, especially when he smiled, at which times his expression bordered closely on the villainous. His hair was very flat and shiny, save at the ends, where it was brushed stiffly up from a low protruding forehead, which assorted well with his harsh voice and coarse manner. He was about two or three and fifty, and a trifle below the middle size; he wore a white neckerchief with long ends, and a suit of scholastic black, but his coat sleeves being a great deal too long, and his trousers a great deal too short, he appeared ill at ease in his clothes, and as if he were in a perpetual state of astonishment at finding himself so respectable.'

Very much 'drawn from life'.

When Nicholas takes on the job of assistant master at Mr Squeers' establishment, Dotherboys Hall, he becomes even more aware of the terrible circumstances in which the unfortunate boys find themselves. One particular tragic boy called Smike, who had stayed on at the school long after the appropriate age owing to his father never having paid any fees, became the drudge and butt of Mrs Squeers ill temper.

Wackford Squeers takes pride in the outrageous behaviour of his wife towards the boys. Dickens writes of her: ' "A most invaluable woman, that, Nickleby" said Squeers when his consort hurried away pushing the Drudge before her. "Indeed, sir!" observed Nicholas. "I don't know her equal", said Squeers; "I do not know her equal. That woman, Nickleby, is always the same – always the same bustling, lively, active, saving creeture that you see her now". Nicholas sighed voluntarily at the thought of the agreeable domestic prospect thus open to him; but Squeers was fortunately, too much occupied with his own reflections to perceive it. "It's my way to say, when I am up in London," continued Squeers, "that to them boys she's a mother. But she's more than a mother to them, ten times more. She does things for them boys, Nickleby that I don't believe half the mothers going would do for their own sons". "I should think they would not, sir", answered Nicholas. The fact was, that both Mr and Mrs Squeers viewed the boys in the light of their proper and natural enemies; or in other words, they held and considered that their business and profession was to get as much from every boy as could possibly be screwed out of him.'

In addition to his pride in his wife, Squeers takes equal pride in the presentation to Nicholas of the 'school room' and its occupants. "There," said the schoolmaster as they stepped in together; "this is our shop, Nickleby". It was such a crowded scene, and there were so many objects to attract attention, that at first Nicholas stared about him, really without seeing anything at all. By degrees, however, the place resolved itself into a bare and dirty room with a couple of windows, whereof a tenth part might be of glass, the remainder being stopped up with old copy-books and paper. There were a couple of long old rickety desks, cut and notched, and inked and damaged, in every possible way; two or three forms, a detached desk for Squeers, and another for his assistant. The ceiling was supported like that of a barn, by cross beams and rafters, and the walls were so stained and discoloured, that it was impossible to tell whether they had ever been touched with paint or whitewash. But the pupils – the young noblemen! How the last faint traces of hope, the remotest glimmering of any good to be derived from his efforts in this den, faded from the mind of Nicholas as he looked in dismay around! Pale and haggard faces, lank and bony figures, children with the countenances of old men, deformities with irons upon their limbs, boys of stunted growth, and others whose long meagre legs would hardly bear their stooping bodies, all crowded on the view together; there were the bleared eye, the hare-lip, the crooked foot, and every ugliness or distortion that told of unnatural aversion conceived by parents for their offspring, or of young lives which, from the earliest dawn of infancy, had been one horrible endurance of cruelty and neglect. There were little faces which should have been handsome, darkened with the scowl of sullen dogged suffering; there was childhood with the light of its eye quenched, its beauty gone, and its helplessness alone remaining; there were vicious-faced boys brooding, with leaden eyes, like malefactors in a jail; and there were young creatures on whom the sins of their frail parents had descended, weeping even for the mercenary nurses they had known, and, lonesome even in their loneliness. With every kindly sympathy and affection blasted in its birth, with every young and healthy feeling flogged and starved down, with every revengeful passion that can fester in swollen hearts, eating its evil way to their core in silence, what an incipient Hell was breeding there!'

Charles Dickens must have enjoyed being 'Nicholas' and laying into Squeers with Squeers' own cane, thus exorcising his own school days. When Squeers is about to beat the retarded weakly Smike for some trivial reason. Nicholas is compelled to act:

"Have you anything to say?" demanded Squeers again: giving his right arm two or three flourishes to try its power and suppleness. "Stand a little out of the way, Mrs Squeers, my dear; I've hardly got room enough." "Spare me, sir!" cried Smike. "Oh! That's all, is it?" said Squeers. "Yes, I'll flog you within an inch of your life, and spare you that." "Ha, ha, ha." laughed Mrs Squeers, "that's a good 'un." "I was driven to do it," said Smike faintly; and casting another imploring look about him. "Driven to do it, were you?" said Squeers. "Oh! It wasn't your fault; it was mine, I suppose – eh?" "A nasty, ungrateful, pig-headed, brutish, obstinate, sneaking dog," exclaimed Mrs Squeers, taking Smike's head under her arm, and administering a cuff at every epithet; "what does he mean by that?" "Stand aside, my dear," replied Squeers. "We'll try and find out." Mrs Squeers being out of breathe with her exertions, complied. Squeers caught the boy firmly in his grip; one desperate cut had fallen on his body – he was wincing from the lash and uttering a scream of pain – it was raised again, and again about to fall – when Nicholas Nickleby suddenly starting up, cried "Stop!" in a voice that made the rafters ring. "Who cried stop?" said Squeers, turning savagely round. "I," said Nicholas, stepping forward. "This must not go on." "Must not go on!" cried Squeers, almost in a shriek. "No!" thundered Nicholas. Aghast and stupefied by the boldness of the interference, Squeers released his hold of Smike, and falling back a pace or two, gazed upon Nicholas with looks that were positively frightful. "I say must not," repeated Nicholas, nothing daunted; "shall not. I will prevent it." Squeers continued to gaze upon him, with his eyes starting out of his head; but astonishment had actually for the moment bereft him of speech. "You have disregarded all my quiet interference in the miserable lad's behalf," said Nicholas; "returned no answer to the letter in which I begged forgiveness for him, and offered to be responsible that he would remain quietly here.

Don't blame me for this public interference. You have brought it upon yourself; not I." "Sit down, beggar!" screamed Squeers, almost beside himself with rage, and seizing Smike as he spoke. "Wretch," rejoined Nicholas, fiercely, "touch him at your peril! I will not stand by and see it done; my blood is up, and I have the strength of ten such men as you. Look to yourself, for by Heaven I will not spare you, if you drive me on." "Stand back," cried Squeers, brandishing his weapon. "I have a long series of insults to avenge," said Nicholas, flushed with passion; "and my indignation is aggravated by the dastardly cruelties practised on helpless infancy in this foul den. Have a care; for if you do raise the devil within me, the consequences shall fall heavily upon your own head." He had scarcely spoken when Squeers, in a violent outbreak of wrath and with a cry like a howl of a wild beast, spat upon him, and struck him a blow across the face with his instrument of torture, which raised up a bar of livid flesh as it was inflicted. Smarting with the agony of the blow, and concentrating into that one moment all his feelings of rage, scorn, and indignation, Nicholas sprang upon him, wrested the weapon from his hand, and, pinning him by the throat, beat the ruffian till he roared for mercy.' William Shaw became infamous and Squeers lives on as an epitaph of his villainy.

Dickens exposed a system which had enabled the proprietors of these disreputable places to take total control and exploit the boys who were left in their 'care' – their families or guardians wanting to be rid of them for various reasons, and paying little or nothing for their education and keep. Some children were even blinded by neglect.

Dickens' exposure of a wicked system helped to bring about improvement and reform.

Nicholas Nickleby gives Wackford Squeers a taste of his own medicine [from *Nicholas Nickleby*; illustrator 'Phiz']

Dora Spenlow

As a young man, Charles Dickens fell deeply in love with a dizzy young girl, daughter of a Mr and Mrs George Beadnell, who considered their daughter, Maria, was far above Charles's station and tried to discourage the association by eventually sending her away to Paris thus removing her from Charles' influence. The young man was devastated and walked the streets in misery. How fond Maria had been of him is hard to say. Dickens transferred her naïve qualities to the 'child wife' Dora in *David Copperfield.* David worships her and is endlessly tolerant of her lack of commonsense, her carelessness, the burning of food, her general ineptitude. After suffering several days of ruined, inedible meals David remonstrates with the dizzy Dora: ' "My precious wife," said I, "we must be serious sometimes. Come! Sit down on this chair, close beside me! Give me the pencil! There! Now let us talk sensibly. You know, dear'; what a little hand it was to hold, and what a tiny wedding ring it was to see! "You know, my love, it is not exactly comfortable to have to go without one's dinner. Now, is it?" "N-n-no!" replied Dora, faintly. "My love, how you tremble!" "Because I KNOW you're going to scold me," exclaimed Dora, in a piteous voice. "My sweet, I am only going to reason." "Oh, but reasoning is worse than scolding!" exclaimed Dora, in despair. "I didn't marry to be reasoned with. If you meant to reason with such a poor little thing as I am, you ought to have told me so, you cruel boy!" I tried to pacify Dora, but she turned away her face, and shook her curls from side to side, and said, "You cruel, cruel boy!" so I took a few turns up and down the room in my uncertainty, and came back again. "Dora, my darling!" "No, I am not your darling. Because you *must* be sorry that you married me, or else you wouldn't reason with me!" returned Dora. I felt so injured by the inconsequential nature of this charge, that it gave me courage to be grave. "Now, my own Dora," said I, "you are very childish, and are talking nonsense. You must remember, I am sure, that I was obliged to go out yesterday when dinner was half over; and that, the day before, I was made quite unwell by being obliged to eat underdone veal in a hurry; today, I don't dine at all – and I am afraid to say how long we've waited for breakfast – and *then* the water didn't boil. I don't mean to reproach you, my dear, but this is not comfortable." "Oh, you cruel, cruel boy, to say I am a disagreeable wife!" cried Dora. "Now, my dear Dora, you must know that I never said that!" "You said, I wasn't comfortable!" cried Dora. "I said the housekeeping was not comfortable!" "It's exactly the same thing!" cried Dora. And she evidently thought so, for she wept most grievously.'

In the novel Dickens 'kills her off' so that David Copperfield can marry his devoted and eminently sensible Agnes Wickfield.

David Copperfield (Charles) meets Dora (Maria)
[from David Copperfield; illustrator 'Phiz']

Maria Beadnell

Dora Spendlow
[from *David Copperfield*;
illustrator ‘Phiz’]

In 1855, when Charles was in his forties. Maria Beadnell came back into his life. He was at the height of his fame when her letter arrived. Charles recognised the handwriting on the envelope. She was married to a Henry Winter and had two daughters. A riot of heartbreaking memory welled up inside him as he remembered her handwriting. "Twenty-four years vanished like a dream and I opened it with the touch of my young friend *David Copperfield*, when he was in love" wrote Dickens in his reply to Maria. He suggested that his wife Kate should arrange a quiet dinner for her and her husband to join them. He asked her if she had "read in *David Copperfield* a faithful reflection of the passion I had for you and that little bits of Dora touches your old self sometimes and a grace here and there that may be revived in your little girls, years hence, for the bewilderment of some other young lover – though he will never be as terribly in earnest as I and *David Copperfield* were. People used to say to me how pretty it all was and how fanciful it was and how elevated it was above the little foolish loves of every young men and women. But, they little thought what reason I had to know it was true, and nothing more or less".

Maria Beadnell was now forty-five years old, and she had warned him in her letter "I am toothless, fat, old and ugly". Charles refused to accept this. Maria wrote back and suggested they met alone before the yet to be arranged dinner. Charles suggested that she should call on him on a particular Sunday afternoon, when he knew he would be alone. "Remember, I accept all with my whole soul, and reciprocate all", he added passionately. His excitement in anticipating her visit was great.

When she arrived Charles was shocked – he hadn't believed her when she had written that she was fat, toothless and old, but alas it was all too true. What was also shattering was his discovery that Maria's infectious gay little laugh, which so captivated the youthful Charles, had now become a silly giggle. Another unsettling surprise was that this 'fat freak' was "tossing her head with a caricature of her girlish manner", and as Edgar Johnson, the biographer, wrote, "throwing him the most distressing imitations of the old glances, behaved as if this private meeting involved them in some intimate agreement. He felt the most horrible fear that she was expecting him to propose an instantaneous elopement". Charles wrote later that this "grotesque revival of what had been prettily natural to her was now like an attempt to resuscitate an old play when the stage was dusty, when the scenery was faded, when the youthful actors were dead, when the orchestra was empty, when the lights were out".

Dickens as a a young man

David Copperfield
[from *David Copperfield*;
illustrator F. A. Fraser]

Flora Finching

Dickens wrote these words months later in *Little Dorrit*, when Flora Finching was clearly based, at least in part, on the forty-year-old Maria – "Flora, whom he had left a lily had become a peony, but that was not much. Flora, who had seemed enchanting in all she said and thought, was diffuse and silly. That was much. Flora had been spoiled and artless long ago, was determined to be spoiled and artless now. That was a fatal blow". The young girl, who had broken his heart when young no longer existed to Dickens and her grotesque shadow had been exorcised in the character of Flora Finching in *Little Dorrit*.

Little Nell

The greatest influence on Charles romantic nature had been Mary Hogarth, the younger sister of Kate Hogarth, the woman Charles married in 1836. The young Mary came to live with the newlyweds at Furnivals Inn. Charles had married Kate on the rebound from Maria. Ironic that they should both eventually resemble each other so closely. Young Mary was to die tragically young at seventeen from a heart condition. Her death was totally unexpected and Charles was devastated. It was while she was residing at Furnivals Inn, when he was writing the Pickwick Papers, that a bond started to build between Charles and his young sister-in-law. She listened to his ideas and always supported him. Kate, on the other hand was not deeply interested in his work and was always too busy with household affairs and looking after the new baby. So, Charles and Mary Hogarth would be much in each other's company, with Mary encouraging Charles with her enthusiasm for his writing in a manner poor Kate wasn't equipped to emulate.

The family moved to 48 Doughty Street, into a house that is now the headquarters of the Dickens Fellowship. Returning one night from a visit to the theatre Charles, Kate and Mary were in excellent spirits. Mary said she was just going to run upstairs to remove her cloak. A few moments later, Kate and Charles heard a cry from upstairs, followed by a thud. Charles dashed upstairs, followed by Kate, only to find Mary lying on her bedroom floor. Together they put the unconscious Mary onto her bed. Charles sat by her bedside holding her hand until the following day, when she died in his arms. Charles wrote that " she sank under the attack and died - died in such a calm and gentle sleep that although I held her in my arms for sometime before, she was certainly living (for she swallowed a little brandy from my hand) I continued to support her lifeless form, long after her soul had fled to heaven. This was about three o'clock on the Sunday afternoon (the next day); they think her heart was diseased. It matters little to relate these details now, for the light and life of our happy circle is gone – and such a blank created as we can never supply". Charles took a ring from Mary's lifeless finger and put it on his own, and it remained there until the day he died. Charles wrote, on the day after her death, "You cannot conceive the misery in which this dreadful event has plunged us. Since our marriage

Maria Beadnell

Flora Finching

she has been the peace and life of our home – the admired of all for her beauty and excellence – I could have better spared a much nearer relation or an older friend, for what she has been to us what we can never replace, and has left a blank which no one who ever knew her can have the faintest hope of seeing supplied".

For some weeks he was unable to work. He wrote to a friend "thank God she died in my arms, and the very last words she whispered were of me. I have lost the dearest friend I ever had. Words cannot describe the pride I felt in her, and the devoted attachment I bore her. She well deserved it for with abilities far beyond her years, with every attraction of youth and beauty, and conscious as she must have been of everybody's admiration, she had not a single fault".

For ever after, Mary became the inspiration and embodiment of Dickens' young heroines. Two years later in the *Old Curiosity Shop* Mary became the character of Little Nell. The death he had planned for his child heroine was so painful that the public wrote in, in large numbers, pleading "Don't let Little Nellie die!" He wrote to his great friend and biographer, John Forster, "I am the wretchedest of the wretched. It casts the most horrible shadow upon me, and it is as much as I can do to keep it moving at all. Nobody will miss Nell, as I will, it is such a very painful thing to me, that I really cannot express my sorrow. Old wounds bleed afresh when I only think of the way of doing it: what the actual doing of it will be God knows… Dear Mary died yesterday, when I think of this sad story." His experience of Mary's death he transferred to Little Nell: 'For she was dead there, upon her little bed, she lay at rest. The solemn stillness was no marvel now. She was dead. No sleep so beautiful and calm, so free from trace of pain, so fair to look upon. She seemed a creature fresh from the hand of God, and waiting for the breath of life; not one who had lived and suffered death. Her couch was dressed with here and there some winter berries and green leaves, gathered in a spot she had been used to favour. "When I die, put near me something that has the loved the light, and had the sky above it always." Those were her words. She was dead. Dear, gentle, patient, noble Nell was dead. Her little bird, a poor slight thing the pressure of a finger would have crushed – was stirring nimbly in its cage; and the strong heart of its child-mistress was mute and motionless for ever.' Further elements of Mary were to be revealed in Dickens' novels yet to come.

Dickens, Mary Hogarth, and his wife, Kate, as drawn by Maclise

The death of Little Nell
[illustrator G. Cattermole]

Mary Hogarth

1

Little Nell

Ebenezer Scrooge

In 1843, Dickens's *Martin Chuzzlewit*, was not as well received as the author had hoped. His disappointment and the fact that his household expenses were getting out of hand drove him to write a new book starting in October, to be on sale for Christmas. This is a tall order for any writer, but only a genius, like Dickens could have produced a masterpiece in time. *A Christmas Carol* was completed, astonishingly, in only six weeks. Dickens insisted that the price of the book be fixed at a popular five shillings (25p today). Needing a plot in a hurry, the resourceful Dickens returned to an old story within a story.

In his first novel *The Pickwick Papers* , at a Christmas party Mr Wardle tells what was said to be an old folk story, concerning Gabriel Grub, a sexton, who was spirited away by goblins on Christmas Eve. Grub was a very disagreeable curmudgeon, whose redemption results from his encounter with goblins.

When two gentlemen visit Scrooge on Christmas Eve, collecting for the poor, Scrooge growls - "Are there no prisons, and the union workhouses, are they still in operation?" The answer comes - "They are still, and I wished that I could say they were not". Scrooge continues "The treadmill and the poor law, are they in full vigour, then?" – "Both are very busy, sir", a gentleman replies. "Oh!" cried Scrooge. "I was afraid, from what you said at first, that something had occurred to stop them in their useful course, I am very glad to hear it!" What a terrible old skinflint Dickens painted. "Oh! But what a tight-fisted hand on the grindstone. Scrooge! A squeezing, wrenching, grasping, scraping, clutching, covetous, old sinner! Hard and sharp as flint, from which no steel had ever struck out generous fire; secret, and self-contained, and solitary as an oyster. The cold within him froze his old features, nipped his pointed nose, shrivelled his cheek, stiffened his gait; made his eyes red, his thin lips blue; and spoke out shrewdly in his grating voice. A frosty rime was on his head, and on his eyebrows, and his wiry chin. He carried his own low temperature always about with him; he iced his office in the dog days and didn't thaw it one degree at Christmas."

Scrooge's conversion came after a visit on Christmas Eve by the ghost of his old dead partner, Jacob Marley. Jacob Marley had led an equally miserly life. 'When the ghost appears Scrooge notices that: 'attached to him was a chain; it was long and wound about him like a tail; it was made up of cash-boxes, keys, padlocks, ledgers, deeds and heavy purses wrought of steel.'

"At this time of the rolling year," the spectre said, "I suffer most. Why did I walk through crowds of fellow beings with my eyes turned down, and never raise them to that blessed star which lead the Wise Men to a poor abode? Were there no poor homes to which its light would have conducted *me*?" "I am here tonight to warn you that you have yet a chance and hope of escaping my fate. A chance and hope of my procuring, Ebenezer". "You were always a good friend to me," said Scrooge. "Thankee!"

"You'll be haunted," resumed the ghost of Jacob Marley, "by three spirits, without their visits you cannot hope to shun the path I tread. Expect the first tomorrow when the bell tolls one. Expect the second on the next night at the same hour. The third, upon the next night when the last stroke of twelve has ceased to

Gabriel Grub, the miserly sexton, being visited by and told the error of his ways by the Chief Goblin on Christmas Eve.
[from *Pickwick Papers*, 1837; illustrator 'Phiz']

Ebenezer Scrooge, the miser, being visited by and told the error of his ways by Marley's Ghost, on Christmas Eve.
[from *A Christmas Carol*, 1843; illustrator Fred Barnard]

vibrate. Look to see me no more; and look that, for your own sake, you remember what has passed between us!" As the story unfolds the three spirits show him the error of his ways and in doing so gave Dickens the opportunity to highlight the social problems and attitudes of his age.

Dickens knew of a man who was called 'the meanest man on earth' - Daniel Dancer – was his name, a miser, who lived in the late eighteenth century, in Harrow Weald, not far from my own home, strangely enough!

Daniel Dancer was the eldest son of a wealthy farmer. When he inherited the estate he could not bring himself to spend any money on the upkeep of the farm, so that in time the house and the farm buildings fell into great disrepair. He never had any fires and he heated his food by covering it and sitting on it until warm enough – not very effective, I suspect. Stories of his hidden wealth circulated widely, and when he died much money was found hidden in an unexpected places all over his ramshackle house. Six hundred pounds was discovered in a cracked teacup, two hundred pounds up the chimney (another good reason not to light a cosy fire) and two thousand five hundred pounds was forked out of a dung heap, all considerable sums in those days.

Scrooge's attitude towards the use of fires was hardly an improvement over that of Daniel Dancer: 'The door of Scrooge's counting-house was open that he might keep his eye upon his clerk, who in a dismal little cell beyond, a sort of tank, was copying letters. Scrooge had a very small fire, but the clerk's fire was so very much smaller that it looked like one coal. But he couldn't replenish it, for Scrooge kept the coal box in his own room; and so surely as the clerk came in with the shovel, the master predicted that it would be necessary for them to part. Wherefore the clerk put on his white comforter, and tried to warm himself at the candle; in which effort, not being a man of strong imagination he failed.' Dickens's wit makes even the most miserly anecdote attractive and amusing.

Dickens combined the misers, the real Daniel Dancer and the fictional Gabriel Grub to produce a character who would survive in world literature as the epitome of a skinflint, Ebenezer Scrooge.

Miser, Daniel Dancer

Gabriel Grub with the Chief Goblin
Illustration from *Pickwick Papers*

Scrooge, from John Leech's illustration

Estella and Miss Havisham

The novelist Wilkie Collins was a close friend of Dickens. In fact Dickens had given Collins's career a great boost by publishing his two best known books *The Moonstone* and *The Woman In White* in a monthly magazine which Dickens edited called *All The Year Round.* In this publication Dickens also first published some of his own novels in monthly parts, such as *Our Mutual friend, A Tale of Two Cities*, etc. Wilkie would tempt Charles to accompany him on unrestrained holidays, sometimes to Paris, where they both let their hair down. They both took part enthusiastically in amateur theatrical productions for charity, which Charles so enjoyed organising. In fact Charles was a very accomplished actor.

The great Victorian actor Macready stated that, in his opinion, Dickens was "the finest actor he had ever seen." When Dickens started to perform his amateur theatrical productions, most of the Dickens family took part in some way or other, joining professional actors. At an audition Charles first set eyes on the eighteen-year-old Ellen Ternan. She was sitting on a property basket, and the profile of her face made an immediate impression on the author. The likeness to his dear, dead Mary was striking. Wilkie Collins witnessed their first meeting and later remarked upon the effect this backstage encounter had on Charles. (Ellen Ternan's mother was also a professional actress. The production of the play *The Frozen Deep* was a great success).

The Dickens marriage had been collapsing for some time. Charles told his close friend John Forster "Poor Katherine and I are not made for each other, and there is no help for it. It is not only that she makes me uneasy and unhappy, but that I make her so too – and much more so. She is exactly what you know, in the way of being amiable and complying; but we are strangely ill-assorted for the bond there is between us. God knows she would have been a thousand times happier if she had married another kind of man, and that her avoidance of this destiny would have been at least equally good for us both. I am often cut to the heart by thinking of what a pity it is, for her own sake, that I ever fell in her way".

Rehearsals for various performances were progressing. During one such process Ellen was being fitted for her part in a rather revealingly brief cotton costume. She may well have been seeking to create a good impression on Dickens. Wilkie Collins was suspicious of Ellen's intentions "I wouldn't have anything to do with her', he warned Charles. "It's no trouble to fall in love", Dickens replied. Collins retorted "It's trouble enough to get out of it once you're in it. So, I keep out of it all together, it would be better for you if you did the same".

But it was too late. The great romantic was 'enslaved' by Ellen. "You have no idea how intensely I love her". He visited the home she shared with her mother, just off the Hampstead Road. Dickens and Ellen sang duets together. Charles had by now started to write *Great Expectations*, and Ellen's increasing coldness was greatly to influence Charles's drawing of Estella's character. He excuses Estella's heartlessness on the grounds that she was brought up by the eccentric and embittered Miss Havisham. Years before, Dickens had heard tell of an eccentric old lady who used to wander aimlessly around the Berners Street area of central London wearing a

Ellen Ternan

Pip and Estella
[illustrator Marcus Stone]

frayed and ragged old wedding dress. Who was this lost creature in an uncaring city? The story, off-told, was that she had once been jilted at the altar, and that public humiliation had turned her mind. Through Dickens's magical imagination she grew into Miss Havisham, dusty and decaying in her increasingly threadbare wedding clothes in *Great Expectations*.

Pip and Miss Havisham
[illustrator Marcus Stone]

Dickens describes young Pip's first encounter with Miss Havisham:

'In an armchair, with an elbow resting on the table, and her head leaning on that hand, sat the strangest lady I have ever seen, or shall ever see.

She was dressed in rich materials – satins, and lace, and silks – all of white. Her shoes were white. And she had a long white veil dependant from her hair, and she had bridal flowers in her hair, but her hair was white. Some bright jewels sparkled on her neck and on her hands, and some other jewels lay sparkling on the table. Dresses, less splendid than the dress she wore, and half-packed trunks, were scattered about. She had not quite finished dressing, for she had but one shoe on – the other was on the table near her hand – her veil was but half arranged, her watch and chain were not put on, and some lace for her bosom lay with those trinkets, and with her handkerchief, and gloves, and some flowers, and a Prayer-book, all confusedly heaped about the looking-glass.'

Through the character of Pip Dickens relives parts of his own experience as he did with the characters of David Copperfield and Nicholas Nickleby.

The hero Pip, like Dickens himself, is unhappy in his unrequited love as Charles pursued Ellen but is not certain at what stage she may have given way to him. But his love was never to be truly reciprocated. The desolation he had experienced with the young Maria and the idealised virtues of Mary Hogarth, still haunted him. He was not to find the solace of a youthful, tender understanding he so yearned for. As their liaison deepened, initially, Ellen was flattered to be the object of the affections of the most famous living writer. The world was at his feet. But it was not a happy relationship, and aside from the difference in their ages, Ellen couldn't reciprocate his overpowering obsession with her. It did not help that Ellen and her mother pressed Charles for money. He bought a house for them, which he added to the already heavy burden of maintaining one house in the country, Gad's Hill, and another in London. The strain on Charles was beginning to take its toll. To support his financial commitments he undertook another rewarding but exhausting tour, including America, of his dramatic readings. Included in his repertoire were extracts from Great Expectations, where he was able, through the words of Pip talking to Estella, to give full reign to his misery over his failing relationship with Ellen:

"..'Come', said Estella. 'You'll get me out of your thoughts in a week.' 'Out of my thoughts. You are part of my existence, part of myself', said Pip. 'You have been in every line I have ever read since I first came here, the rough, common boy, whose poor heart you wounded even then. You have been in every prospect I have seen since, on the river, on the sails of ships, on the marshes, in the clouds, in the light, in the darkness, in the wind, in the woods, in the sea, in the street - … you have been the embodiment of every graceful fancy that my mind has ever become acquainted with'."

The tour finally took its toll, and after a reading at St. James's Hall in London, Charles Dickens collapsed. Until recently, it has been accepted that Dickens died at his home, Gad's Hill. But a more dramatic and more appropriate account of the passing of the great storyteller came to light a few years ago. It seems that Charles had died at the little house he had bought for Ellen. She and her mother were anxious to suppress the scandal that would surely have ensued. They concocted a plot as mysterious and dramatic as any created by Dickens. With the connivance of the Dickens family, the body was taken to Gad's Hill by carriage, by the light of the moon. It was a fitting end to the story of a man who all his life had concocted dramatic tales and mysteries. Truth can sometimes be as dramatic as the extravagances of the imagination. This is a conclusion, I think, which can be equally applied to the other stories in this book about the characters that have been 'drawn from life'.

Dickens in 1867

“What?” said Estella, preserving her attitude of indifference as she leaned against the great chimney-piece, and only moving her eyes. Do you reproach me for being cold? You!”
[illustrator F. A. Fraser]

INDEX

INDEX